DEEPLY WO

"In his inspiring book, *Deeply Woven Roots*, Gary Gunderson has done a remarkable job in clarifying the balance between law and gospel, faith and action. He has a deep love and respect for the power of the congregation. He convincingly describes how the churches of America can and do serve as 'health centers,' bringing health and healing to thousands of communities. This is preventive medicine for whole persons at its best."

—GRANGER WESTBERG
AUTHOR OF GOOD GRIEF

"This book confirms my 25-year experience with hundreds of religion-related counseling centers. Congregations can provide a structure for health care that is both cost-effective and healing in and of itself."

—R. J. ROSS
FOUNDER/PRESIDENT
THE SAMARITAN INSTITUTE

"The storytelling, the concrete approach, and the faith basis for acting to bring about systemic change make this book not only easy reading but a challenge to the reader to think differently. Gunderson's emphasis on 'healthier communities' startles us as individuals to recognize that we are a society in pain and that a relational approach is not only apt but necessary. I recommend this work wholeheartedly, for it approaches the need of society through the 'gospel lens' to be Jesus in our times."

—MARGARET MARY KIMMINS, O.S.F.
GENERAL MINISTER
FRANCISCAN SISTERS OF ALLEGHENY

DEEPLY
WOVEN
ROOTS

Improving the Quality of Life
in Your Community

GARY GUNDERSON

Fortress Press
Minneapolis

DEEPLY WOVEN ROOTS
Improving the Quality of Life in Your Community

Scripture quotations from the New Revised Standard Version of the Bible are copyright © 1989 by the Division of Christian Education of the National Council of Churches of Christ in the United States of America and are used by permission. Scripture quotations from the Holy Bible, New International Version, are copyright © 1973, 1978, 1984 by International Bible Society. Used by permission of Zondervan Publishing House. All rights reserved. The "NIV" and "New International Version" trademarks are registered in the United States Patent and Trademark Office by International Bible Society. Use of either trademark requires the permission of International Bible Society.

Book and cover design by Joseph Bonyata.

Cover art: *Etude Pour un Paysage*, Fernand Léger, copyright © 1997 Artists Rights Society (ARS), New York / ADAGP, Paris. Used by permission.
Author photo: Annemarie Poyo, copyright © Emory University Photography.

Library of Congress Cataloging-in-Publication Data

Gunderson, Gary
    Deeply Woven Roots : improving the quality of life in your
community / Gary Gunderson
        p.   cm.
    Includes bibliographic references.
    ISBN 0-8006-3095-5 (alk. paper)
    1. Church. 2. Church and the World. 3. Mission of the church.
    4. Church and social problems. I. Title
    BV600.2.G86 1997
    261.8—dc21   97-35285
                                                                         CIP

The paper used in this publication meets the minimum requirements of American National Standard for Information Sciences—Permanence of Paper for Printed Library Materials, ANSI Z329.48-1984.

Manufactured in the U.S.A.   AF 1-3095

01   00   99   98   97   1   2   3   4   5   6   7   8   9   10

CONTENTS

ACKNOWLEDGMENTS

THIS BOOK GROWS FROM THE RICHLY DEMONSTRATED faith and intelligence of my colleagues in the Interfaith Health Program and in the many, many projects I've been able to experience and witness around the country. Thank you.

I want to acknowledge my debt to my wife, Karen, who encouraged me, and to my editor, Michael West, who gracefully helped me.

I have a special gratitude to two laypeople whose lives push the envelope of possibility a little further in a hopeful direction every day, Dr. Bill Foege and President Jimmy Carter.

I hope this book honors the lives of my parents, Beatrice and Roy Gunderson, who taught me before I knew I was learning about what endures: faith, hope, and the greatest, love.

PREFACE

I RECOILED FROM THE PHONE AS FROM POISON, instinctively fearing the death to be contagious, infecting my own child too. Mark was the only son of John and Susan, a good kid, a friend. His car had left the road, impacting an oak and killing him. Mark had been finishing up errands before going to see his grandparents in Texas. His plane ticket lay on the front seat. Maybe he had forgotten his insulin, maybe he had just looked away at the wrong time. No matter. He was dead; and his family, church, and every parent who heard the news reeled.

Karen and I were well into our fifth pregnancy, which so far had produced our daughter Lauren and three miscarriages. We knew the slender line between life and death. I had almost decided to avoid Mark's funeral altogether when one of the Oakhurst deacons called and asked me to deliver the prayer in the funeral service. The question was not whether I could pray for John and Susan and Mark. It was could I pray at all.

Oakhurst Baptist Church has long been a safe place for doubters to pray and grievers to mourn. On that weekday morning the yellow light streaming through the high windows washed over old oak pews filled with people who could barely make eye contact for fear of betraying their doubt. Sitting in the middle of the congregation were John and

Susan, choosing to be surrounded, not set apart, in their grief—part of a congregation of loss.

I was glad that I had only to pray and not to preach. "Oh, Parent God," I prayed, "you have lost a son too. Teach us how to cry and how to give thanks when the tears are dry again. You must make us strong but not strong as individuals—strong as a family. Some of us need to be silent; others need to cry out loud. But none of us needs to be alone. We must experience you among us now, filling the gaps and silences between us, or the death and the horror will freeze us cold. And we will be alone.

"God, we have been here before and secretly trusted our learning, our cleverness, and our money. But these are dust to us today. We pray to you because there is no other. And we know these are the prayers you want to answer, for you love us like a daddy, like a mommy. And we need you."

God was in that place that day. But we knew it might take more than a lifetime for all of the prayer to be answered. Even then the complexity and ambiguity that define human experience will not be wrapped up, understood, complete. But we prayed and sang and wept. Together.

Only later during a long, bitter, and public divorce proceeding did we begin to understand the ironic pain that had filled the sanctuary, the deep wound that had fractured that family long before Mark's car hit the tree. John had told Susan only a few weeks earlier that he had been gay for years and now was HIV-positive. Their marriage had blown apart, and amid flying pieces, Mark had moved in with a church friend rather than stay in the tension.

Some praying that day are now dead—of AIDS, age, and other car wrecks. And what was then our fragile pregnancy is now Kathryn, whom we brought into the same congregational space where we had prayed at Mark's death. Deacon Jim Brooks held her high above his head in his strong, gentle hands and offered her up to the congregation, the congregation to her, and the new relationship between them to God. "Little Kathryn, long before you can know our names, we know yours; you are already part of us—this congregation—and we love you."

Congregations Shaping Communities

This is a book about how congregations can and should and do shape communities across North America at the dawn of the twenty-first century. But it seems important to say early on that my writing is in no sense objective for I have been formed by my particular congregation, which meets at the corner of East Lake Drive and Third Avenue in an otherwise nondescript neighborhood in Decatur, Georgia. When I think of congregations, I do not think first of national patterns. It is the other way around, in fact. I think first of this *particular* place, where tears have been shed and hopes quickened, children buried and others raised up high. This has surely ground the lens through which I have been able to see the strengths of other congregations in other communities.

My own peculiar place of faith is of Baptist tradition, although many Baptists might have trouble recognizing it now. It is important to say quickly that the essential strength of congregations is expressed in those groups growing out of many traditions, including many kinds of Christians, Buddhists, Jews, and Muslims. This is not to say that those theological differences are irrelevant or that we are becoming the same. Theological language is urgently needed in order for us to engage and understand our times. But the intellectual engagement must proceed from the experience of engaging in the life found in an actual congregation of human beings engaged in all that it means to serve and celebrate at a real address on a particular street corner. Interfaith dialogues often sound like paleontologists comparing life forms found in bedrock shale at the bottom of the Grand Canyon. This book attempts to look at some of the living life forms on the streets. On those streets it is clear that the real contest is not between different faiths, but between those with faith and those in despair. Abraham Heschel once said that we must choose between "interfaith and inter-nihilism."[1]

A remarkable issue of the *Journal of Social Issues* that examined the role of religion on health concluded that "religious beliefs and institutions can foster prejudice or inhibit it; enhance family cohesiveness or destroy it; encourage copying activity or suppress it; and/or provide a life perspective of hope and optimism, or of fear and resentment.

Understanding the role of religion with respect to any particular problem requires a highly differentiated view of both religion and the problem under consideration, as well as a coherent model of their interrelations. The devil, so to speak, is in the details."[2] Much research points to positive links between congregations as stable, long-term, preventive resources for families, youth, and adults. But little research has examined the specific features of congregations that facilitate this.[3] This book may shed some light on that.

I am grounded in the particular experience of being in one congregation for more than twenty years, which is mostly why this is a simple hopeful book. First we'll explore some of the drivers of congregational change today, their larger context in social and health dynamics. In my work at the Carter Center I am frequently called on by secular and governmental organizations to help them figure out how to relate to religious groups. Many such organizations, driven partly by funding constraints and partly by frustration over the difficulty of making communities behave, are turning toward faith-based organizations for help. Although they want a simple model for engagement, I resist turning collaboration into a mechanical exercise, as if one could just negotiate access to spare buildings and volunteers. I found myself trying to explain the need to look beyond the temporary structures to the underlying strengths inherent in religious congregations. In effect, to look beneath the uniform, to the muscle, bone, and heart. I believe the new patterns of collaboration emerging among social institutions, including government, religious, private, voluntary, and for-profit organizations, reflect deep and enduring shifts in social currents. Many of the decisions have become urgent due to irresponsibly short-sighted actions, especially by government. However, it is still critical that the renegotiation of these roles rests on the consideration of underlying strengths, not just short-term political expediency. Some of the assets of religious organizations are "inconvenient strengths" in that they are more rich and complex than a bureaucrat in a hurry may want to understand. Nevertheless, enduring shifts in relationships must eventually rest on strengths and that will take time sooner or later to see clearly.

How then does a congregation have the strength to pour itself out for the community? Like most living phenomena, it is almost impossibly complex to engineer. Fortunately, this is an organic process to be nurtured, not a machine to be engineered. Think like a gardener, and it becomes easier to see. It happens—is happening—in communities of every sort and size.

For more than 20 years I've traveled around the United States and Africa constantly delighted by the astonishing collaborative efforts that spring up when people act on their faith and compassion. Three years ago colleagues with the Interfaith Health Program and I went to more than 20 communities around the U.S. including St. Louis; Dallas; Baltimore; Tacoma; Los Angeles; Aiken, South Carolina; Columbus, Ohio; Portland; Oakland; Baltimore; Memphis; Minneapolis; Tucson; Columbia; Chicago; and Newark. We met in groups ranging in size from twenty to forty-five people. We met on campuses and in city hall basements, churches, and hospitals. These were leaders who have their hands on the problem, those who have devoted themselves to realizing the opportunities for tangible increase in the health of their communities.

We found there is no problem that some group somewhere is not successfully engaged in. At a time when so many are fearful and anxious for the future, this is remarkable. Cancer, the ozone, random violence, poverty, HIV, grinding stress, and rising costs of health care fill us with the dull sense that it is only a matter of time until it all collapses. Many look toward faith to serve as an anchor to slow the drift into social catastrophe, to hold onto the past. We met people living out a quite different kind of faith—one that begins with the assumption that God is driving us forward, and the very structure of the created universe beckons us to seize opportunities for better health and wholeness. They lean into the future with expectation.

This book is weighted more toward the religious turn of phrase, as opposed to those more common in the health sciences. That is because the faith and health movement must take off primarily from the faith structures, or it will not move at all. But I do not intend to lend any support to those who would seek to replace government with religious providers or replace hard-won protections from religious abuse by mere expediency.[4] The challenges and opportunities demand something much richer and stronger. Let me sketch what I mean by "the movement." The movement to bring congregational resources to bear on society's deepest problems—especially public health and poverty—connects religious communities to their larger communities at the roots. It is a twinning of anger and hope. Such anger is grounded in the fact that the more than two-thirds of all years of human life lost before the age of sixty-five are lost unnecessarily to preventable causes. It is outrageous that many of these lost years result from organized greed—some legal (as in the tobacco and handgun industries), some illegal (as with substance abuse). People are unnecessarily wasting their lives and even dying due to apathy, ignorance, and habit. Public health science fuels this anger because it has clarified what can now be done to eliminate the suffering.

Social Need Meets Religious Imperative

A movement isn't a movement until it has a common idea. The faith-and-health movement reflects an idea underlying much contemporary health science, which tells us that no magic bullet, no one pill or plan, no one action is capable of bringing health to a community. There is no way to fix all problems, cure all diseases, or patch up all injuries. The movement is instead about prevention and connection. It is not defined by what we can do by ourselves but by what we must do together. This fact shapes our strategy and the tools we choose.

Those of us in the religious community should feel embarrassment and shame at the state of health in our society. For too long we have drifted with the tide, accepting the failure to feed and immunize children, confront gunrunners and tobacco pushers, and stop environmental abuse. We should be outraged that the mentally ill could remain outside the range of health-care reform. Our faith traditions challenge us with the knowledge that this is not what God intends. We have drifted with the apathetic tide when we could have been doing far more. Our faith and our science both compel us to seize the moment and work together because it is the right thing to do.

We have instead largely abandoned the language of public faith to those who would harness God as they might an old horse, in hopes that it would pull us back to an imaginary past, away from all that makes us uncomfortable with our present and all that we fear about the future. I want that language back, and I want those who care about the health of the public—of their communities—to recognize that language as their friend.

I originally developed this line of thought for those outside religious structures. I found that those on the outside were, if anything, quicker to understand the opportunity than leaders inside. When asked what their church or synagogue did, those inside tended to run off the list of scheduled activities: "We do Sunday school at 9:30, worship at 11:00, the food pantry is open on Tuesday and Thursday, the tutoring and respite care programs on the other days." It is hard to step back from one's own structure to see its underlying strengths and especially to think of how they might be radically transformed in service to a new menu of opportunities and needs in the community. That is exactly what I hope to do here. This is not a dream spun out of imaginary thread. Rather, it is woven from the lives of my own congregation, the many clergy and laypeople I have met around the nation through my work at Seeds and the Carter Center. It is probably happening near you, too. Once you know the strengths to look for, they are hard to miss.

CHAPTER 1
DEEPLY WOVEN ROOTS

A very uncertain congregation then looks across an unfamiliar mission frontier to an environment that appears less and less friendly and wonders. It often discovers ambiguities from the environment have migrated into the congregation itself. It wonders how to constitute itself for the new mission that the new world calls for. It wonders what good news it has, how to deliver it, and to whom. It wonders how to differentiate itself from its environment.[5]

—Loren Mead, Alban Institute

AMID TODAY'S DISORIENTATION AT THE congregational level lie many hopeful clues of the emerging future. The church does not choose its own future. Rather, it is formed in the creative tension between the actuality of the human situation and the intentions of God. Many in the churches focus on how to strengthen the congregation for their own survival over against a cultural drift they fear. This book asks a quite different question: What is the role of faith in forming and sustaining human communities that are healthy, that reflect God's intentions? If there is any hope at all, it is that God intends the renewal of the whole world. Congregations are a tool for that greater purpose, not themselves the point.

Not Survival but Service

As a practical matter, the continued survival of religious congregations is dependent not so much on their defensive strengths against the world but on how their inherent strengths are useful in realizing God's hope for human communities. All the organizational cleverness of all the brightest committees will be useless if the congregation is not aligned with what God hopes to do in the community. This is not easy to see in a time of radical change, especially because much of the change within and without the congregation affects how we connect to each other—how we produce, buy, sell, learn, ask, and help and heal one another. The congregation is just one more place where people are connected to each other, one more field of connections that is changing. We are tempted to think in terms of marketing or positioning and miss the whole point. Congregations are where people come together, gathered by God to serve God's intentions of renewing and redeeming the whole world, not in domination but in love. So often we religious people turn the *appearance* of love and service into a marketable commodity in exactly the same way that the most crass "health" companies cynically market their services.

In a practical Monday-morning kind of way, how do we know what to do next? Where do we allocate our slender store of time and money and people, toward exactly which activities and events? To answer the questions, we must understand the underlying strengths of congregations that are most relevant to the enduring needs of our times. The precise way those strengths and needs intersect will constantly shift; and the precise activities, events, and physical structures will shift with them. But if we understand our underlying strengths and move in faith toward our deepest sense of God's hope, we can move in confidence. We must begin by understanding the relevant strengths of religious communities in this new day so that we can play toward them and build on them for the sake of the larger community.

The Language of Health

It is hard for many of us to get beyond our personal fears to find assurance in a God who cares about *communities* and moves through *congregations*. The Carter Center engages members of many faith traditions across the nation with opportunities to build communities using the framework of health. Our interest is in communities, which are not just the aggregate experience of all the individuals inside some arbitrary boundaries. In our popular culture we tend to think of health as something that happens to individuals, not to communities. We have difficulty speaking about communities in anything other than the language of mechanical functions and services. The language of health initially seems odd because we have removed the word from its roots in relationship—wholeness—and, quite literally, privatized it, even *monetized* it. Health is one more commodity to be purchased and consumed by individuals. You would think religious groups would know better than that. In recent decades religious organizations have found themselves in control of vast health organizations worth many billions of dollars. Given this extraordinary accumulation of ministry assets, one would think congregations would be fairly sophisticated in health vocabulary. The opposite is true. Most congregations, if they think about it at all, see health as "somebody else's specialty" beyond the capacity or qualifications of a mere congregation to address. So on one hand, health is a language to describe purely private matters. And on the other hand, it is a language we too quickly relinquish to specialists with complex tools at their command. The language is worth taking back.

Jesus, who ministered long before antibiotics, stainless steel, or health insurance were invented, spent at least a third of his time in healing ministry. Martin Marty, speaking at the Carter Center 1989 Conference on the Church's Challenge in Health, suggests that Jesus spent *three-thirds* in healing, if you include the linkages of mental and spiritual distress in healing.[6] It is exactly this missing two-thirds that we seek to reclaim and to reintroduce into the discussion concerning the role of faith structures in building community. This is not only necessary to make a place for the church in health, but to breathe life back into what has become a barren, technical language. Faith needs the language of health in order to understand how it applies to life; health needs the language of faith in order to find its larger context, its meaning.

The language of health must compete with that of economics to describe our communities. It often loses the contest to the point where health itself is dumbed down to mean simply what services people can buy. But even at its most primitive level of reporting on physical status (such as average birth weights, hospital admissions, rates of immunization, disease, and life expectancy), health language at least attempts to describe qualities of life, pain, and ability to function. The language of money measures only the ability to pay for things that may not actually bear on anyone's life. Money is always an intermediate good that has to be exchanged for something of more direct value in order to mean anything at all. Health language lets us move closer to the human experience to talk about what matters, what hurts. Moreover, it is a language that helps us describe and see our communities.

Sickly Roots

The ultimate context of health and health care is religious. Many communities are broken apart, fractured from each other, confused, and incoherent. This shows up in public trends as increasing polarization among racially defined groups and specialized interests. It shows up at the individual level as health indicators related to stress, bad life choices, and self-destructive behavior. The root health problem is alienation and meaninglessness, which can hardly be solved with self-help techniques, even the spiritual ones that line bookstore shelves these days. Isolation of the self is the problem and cannot be the locus of the answer.

Walter Brueggemann notes that even the church has tended to respond to isolation with a ministry of accommodation, helping people to adjust to the negative byproducts of too much autonomy. This calls, not for some minor tinkering around, but for a deep transformation. Much of this work in the churches rests on those who do pastoral care. Brueggemann warns that "Pastoral care will have the capacity to join such an issue only as it is intentionally grounded in and authorized by a truth claim that is based outside our cultural values."[7]

At the core of every major faith tradition stands an explicit commitment to be with the sick, the poor, the alienated, the marginal, the wounded, and the dying. The commitments are very old, but the implications are forever new and increasingly radical because of remarkable changes in health science. But what faith group has begun to live up to their potential as agents to prevent suffering? Even a superficial glance at the numbers exposes the ironic comfort of the U.S. faith groups.

When health is regarded as something to be consumed one person at a time, it lies nearly out of the reach of this powerful linkage to faith and justice. This disconnection has been vividly demonstrated in recent years. Churches in America have hardly known what to say as the entire system of health services has been rearranged with scarcely a word of justice spoken. When the voice of justice was raised, it focused overwhelmingly on the payment system that governs what happens when health fails, rather than on the underlying relationships among humans. Health is only partly shaped by what happens between a person and his or her doctor and other specialists. Far more important are the relationships and circumstances whose cumulative weight presses on the person, defining the length and quality of their prospects. Those working within the health system are struggling toward a new understanding of how the systems works together. A high-level group of medical educators convened by the Fetzer Institute and the Pew Charitable Trusts concluded that "It is not a grand machine, a complex of physical facilities, advanced pharmaceuticals, surgical techniques, or an administrative system, however wonderfully conceived. It is instead an essentially human activity, undertaken and given meaning by people in relationships with one another and their communities, both public and professional."[8] Of course, once one has moved from technologies to relationships, one has entered a radically new frame of understanding that turns out to be home base to religion and ethics. Alastair Campbell, writing in the midst of the (eventually aborted) national health care reform debate, frames health around liberation, not therapy.

Health has both personal and social dimensions, each related to the holistic account of health and illness as the fulfillment or frustration of human aspirations and intentions. These dimensions come together in the concept of health as liberation—a setting free which each individual must seek for him or herself but which also requires a transformation of social values and a redistribution of political power.[9]

The broader view of health is emerging not primarily because religious people are calling for it. Indeed, we have been quite comfortable playing out our minor therapeutic role on the sidelines. The drive toward complexity is coming from within the health sciences themselves. A recent landmark study by the Institute of Medicine defined health as a "state of well-being and the capability to function in the face of changing circumstances." Health is, therefore, a positive concept emphasizing social and personal resources as well as physical capabilities. Improving health is a shared responsibility of health care providers, public health officials, and a variety of other actors in the community who can contribute to the well-being of individuals and populations.[10] The report describes a "field model" of health that rests on nine components including the social environment, physical environment, genetic endowment, individual response (behavior and biology), health care, disease, health and function, well-being, and prosperity.[11]

Something in us makes us want to make all this more complicated than it is. The most reliable predictor of a person's long-term health is not access to medical services, but one's educational level, which is best understood as a function of the economic status of one's parents. This is in itself easily oversimplified to mean the capacity to purchase medical services. Rather, it reflects the broad and cumulative impact of privileged access to education, housing, safety, employment, and food. The prophetic eye of faith understands that these privileges are not given unequally by God, but reflect brokenness and sin, compounded over time. Dr. William Foege, Distinguished Professor of Public Health at the Rollins School of Public Health, points out that poverty manifests in health much like a hereditary disease, in that its effects ripple through the generations and that it is also "dose-related" in that its effects and longevity increase with exposure.[12] Swimming against the tide of individualized managed care, public health science continues to point to the fundamental relationship between socioeconomic status and health.[13]

Healthy persons do not just score well in terms of the internal functioning of their own organs, nutritional systems, and muscles. As suggested by the Institute of Medicine, a healthy person is one who is able to play a role in the family, the community, and the whole of created life. So health is not determined by a comparison against arbitrary average scores of some kind. It is best understood as the ability to fulfill many shifting personal roles as the years go by, as life wounds and bruises us and removes and adds people to our social web. This broadens, but does not remove the issue of physical and mental status. Looking at the capacity to participate in human community is the key. This capacity makes description more complex and nuanced, for it beckons us to examine those factors that affect social participation over time. For instance, Raynard Kingston, a senior researcher at the Rand Corporation, has studied how families' wealth and source of income result in different functional capacities decades later.[14] The new broader view of health comes much closer to the old understandings expressed in most faiths.

Individual isolation and its inevitable meaninglessness are linked to disease and pathology of all sorts. As medical science slowly pushes beyond biochemical mechanisms, it finds itself exploring the social and spiritual ground of human health. It finds that, just as one cannot very well fix an elbow without some understanding of the larger organism, so it is difficult to understand an individual's health apart from those things that make the person coherent, whole, meaningful. At times this puts greatest stress on physical indicators, at other times on emotional, mental, or spiritual ones. The emerging view of health even at the individual level is more like ecology, less like mechanics. We find not only links between mind, body, spirit, but interrelationships that make our mechanistic language seem crude and silly.[15] Emily Martin suggests that our radically changing understanding of how our bodies work, especially the idea of a flexible, adaptive immune system, is changing our self understanding at a deep level.[16] All this is to say that linking "health" and "faith" is incendiary, evocative, powerful, much more than just shifting some medical services for the poor from the government to congregations.

Science is unlikely to make additional progress on increasing the average lifespan or quality of life until we develop a far less mechanical, far more humane understanding of how humans are woven together. I think of the time my parents visited when my daughter Lauren was just four years old. My dad had a bad foot at the time and, even though he would have preferred to crawl, we wrestled him into a wheelchair. Lauren thought it was a great honor to pilot him through the crowd at the airport. I carried the luggage while my child parented my parent. This is healthy. We enter and leave in others' care. In between we find ourselves suspended in webs of dependence that we name uncle, father, child, friend, colleague, wife, believer, member, disciple, deacon, follower.

Integrating Spirituality and Health

Science is beginning to realize that faith is part of being a healthy human. Public health scientists document that even such superficial indicators as frequent attendance at religious services have significant links to better health over many years.[17] When we don't have faith—when the world doesn't make sense—our lack of coherence drives us toward destructive behavior in conscious and unconscious ways until that brokenness expresses itself in a way that can be described by the crude measures of health science.

The language of health sharpens our vision of ourselves and those to whom we are connected. Health in itself, however, is only one marker of the mature, fully grown person. Every religion considers long life a secondary virtue, holding its praise for those who share freely of themselves for others. Our highest admiration is reserved for those who lay down their lives for the weak, the persecuted, the children. This is a sign of great spiritual health. The deep paradox at the intersection of faith and health must not be devalued as a mere prescription for personal prosperity and longevity.

At present most of the work on linking spirituality and health reflects our individualistic perspective. We want to harness spirituality like another vitamin or diet scheme for our personal gain. Or we might want to employ it as a therapeutic strategy for individual patients. This works on a limited basis, of course, but it misses the point. The primary gift of spiritual life is not knowledge of one's own private functioning. The great power comes from a sense of finding one's place in the universe and finding that that place is a gift of a gracious God. This puts all things private, including personal health, in a perspective quite different from the dominant one of our society, which urges us to resist death with every penny and every medical trick. What humans actually know is that we are here briefly and die, and in between the only thing that matters is giving and receiving love among other humans. If we do not make sense of that, we are likely to not be very healthy while we are here.

Spirituality is not primarily about longevity but about perspective—understanding where we fit, who we are in relation to everyone and everything else. Integrating spirituality into health strategies will not be like simply adapting another biomechanical tool into the medical kit.

Health is inherently communal. When I was still a young member at Oakhurst, I was asked to pray at the memorial service for one of the longtime members, Carl Couch. I felt like a seedling near a great but fallen oak. Carl had been at Oakhurst for decades, serving on every possible committee, attending every possible event. He was a fully grown man of faith, and his death left a big gap. Of course, Carl did not simply die one day and disappear from our lives. He nurtured our ongoing lives with his memory just as surely as a fallen oak feeds the forest soil and holds the young giants still reaching upward.

It is hard not to look up in awe into the high reaches of a deep and healthy forest. But the true story is in the dirt, the roots. And what is forest loam but fallen trees? Everywhere you look in a natural forest you see trees on their way to loam and soil on its way to the sky.

Ever since that day, I have thought of a congregation and its surrounding community as a forest, an image that leads us into the future in two ways. First, we can see ourselves as one of the trees, taking comfort in the complex richness of our enduring connections. Second, we can see ourselves as foresters, with the humble patience of stewards who measure their contribution in terms of decades, nurturing and defending a living process.

Although a forest may span miles, any one tree has to grow where it happened to sprout, hoping to bear the fruit it can. Storms and fires sweep aside the weak. Some are more resilient than others; some keep growing even after they are knocked down. But the big difference is whom they grow next to, whose roots tangle with their own.

A forest's resilience reflects diversity. Any one tree relies not just on its own roots but on an interwoven fabric of roots. And while it is a good thing to put down roots, grow into the wind, and rise high into the sky, it is also good to know that even in our falling, even as our individual memories slip behind, we will be part of the whole.

Roots Nurtured in Faith

Compared to a human community, a forest is simple because trees have no choice: They neither aspire nor fear. People do not have to grow where they are planted. They can, for a time, totally ignore that which has given them life and refuse their own support to the system. People may be born into a forest, but they have to choose to stay there. The fractious winds of our time have blown many far away from anything that feels like a community at all.

Our task is more complicated and humbling than growing trees. Foresters do not have to persuade the trees in their care to participate in the process. Indeed, sometimes it is harder for foresters to understand that they must work *with* the life in the forest. They do not bring life to the trees and cannot force it to be expressed. In a far more complex way, human communities must choose to allow themselves to be nurtured, to sink roots, to live.

At the Carter Center we frequently work with groups taking on large-scale, complex problems and opportunities. It is common to find an entire coalition clustered around a new (or renamed) technical idea of some kind that will fix a large social problem. Complexity is a constant frustration to such groups, who wish to squeeze life into conveniently packaged to-do lists. The humble-scale congregational life is far beneath the view of most global visionaries. But the future does not flow merely from a compendium of techniques or a toolkit of solutions to problems defined by specialized disciplines. It is born from faith, which makes insights from different disciplines coherent and places technical opportunities in a frame of meaning that justifies and motivates risk.

Where Are the Real Leaders?

Faith in a coherent but open-ended body of thought is essential to hopeful action. Where does hope come from? Where is it formed? Not in private, although private disciplines are essential. Faith is a social gift, just as compassion is a social expression. Faith is formed in a congregation, where it is social, tangible, inconvenient, and real. More specifically, hope is shaped in a group of people who push beyond a general image and words to something specific, nearby, tangible enough to reach out toward—*this* mission and clinic, *that* group of men who need food or a place to stay, *this* neighborhood with kids who need tutoring, *this* member who needs a group home.

Even while writing this manuscript I was pulled away to a conference call with people from around the world strategizing to mobilize global resources to meet the needs of developing countries. I sat, doodling on my notepad in my kitchen, looking out the window at a squirrel on the deck, while I listened by speakerphone to the big people in Washington, D.C. It occurred to me that similar earnest conversations were going on at the time all over the world, some over high-tech phone links, others on the Internet, others in boardrooms and at airport hotels. Sometimes the discussion concerns more local phenomena: schools, the elderly, the homeless. The conversation swings between impending doom—defined by the numbers of youth killing each other or species dying in the Amazon—and astonishing opportunities— usually meaning some technical marvel or organizational scheme.

Inevitably, the discussions turn toward how to get some big-name leader to lend his or her blessing to the movement. We recycled the dozen names that always come up: Mandela, Tutu, Powell, my boss (President Carter), and so on—the same list whether we talk about youth violence or global warming.

Sometimes, when problems relate to inconvenient kinds of people, such as the homeless or African refugees, we seek not a leader but a gullible (if noble) group on which to shift responsibility. In the United States this is often some kind of religious group. The reflex is similar to the one seeking the great leader: Can we persuade somebody else to take responsibility for doing what we know to be the right thing?

Why not just do the right thing ourselves? Why wait for the sanction from some important person before doing the right thing boldly? Even on global issues, just below the dozen brand-name moral leaders are tens of thousands of leaders with great capacity who are increasingly resonating to very similar themes and images of the future. Why remain captive to celebrity, waiting for leaders to catch up?

Those whom one would expect to lead, in fact, express their sense of being driven by forces beyond their capacity to challenge or resist. On a global scale national leaders feel powerless before the demands of capital markets that insist on a policy environment that may have little to do with the best interests of their countries. They are elected to lead but find their choices limited by the need to conform to global standards. But who sets the global standards? Can nobody say no?

In my experience the future is frequently mediated by those who are unqualified, those whose bold hope pulls them across the boundaries of propriety that hold the more credentialed people back. The same is true at the level of communities. Why the violence in our streets and homes? Who is driving the arms race in our neighborhoods? The best estimates say that around 150,000 children come to school armed every day, the vast majority of which report they must do so for their own safety, responding to forces beyond their control. Of course, the ones they fear are armed because they fear someone else. Can nobody say no? Even more importantly, who can say yes?

We are not the first to be able to do the right thing in a relative sense, but the absolute gains now within our grasp are quite without precedent. When the United Methodist bishops committed themselves to a global initiative for children in 1996, they observed:

> Ours is the first generation in history to have the capacity to accomplish what has previously only been imaginable. God, through technicians and scientists, has brought the goals of removing and preventing needless suffering within reach. What is needed is a renewed vision of God's reign of justice, generosity and joy for all people.[18]

For all of recorded human existence, suffering has been well documented, and most religious apology has revolved around explaining why capricious suffering could be part of a just cosmos. But now we know we can inexpensively prevent most causes of premature death. Why do we fail to do so? While once we thought the universe was hardwired for capricious suffering, it now looks as if God has wired the universe for continuous improvement. We know that most of the ongoing causes of disease, injury, and premature death are due to our failure to do things we know how to do.

The Reverend Gerald Durely, pastor of Providence Baptist Church in west Atlanta, tells of meeting with several dozen mothers who had lost their children to gunfire on city streets. They told of going to the emergency rooms alone, then to the morgue seeking their sons. The anguish would never leave them. But their anger was focused on the church: "Where was the Church when I walked alone into that morgue? Where were you when we needed you? Where were you when my son was alone on the street?"

Social Challenge, Faith Challenge

We are in an era of profound social innovation, both driven and pulled by fundamental changes in the technologies that connect us to one another. These systems are the sites in which we grow, make, sell, buy, learn, earn, share, threaten, and help. The technical changes at play today ensure that the future will most likely emerge from places that are surprising and small, that demonstrate new combinations of strength and need. Many of these social innovations rest on voluntary collaboration between people and institutions. The key is that we will take risks only for the ideas that emerge from places fully in touch with human frailty, pain, and limitation—especially the limitation of love and lovelessness, of meaning and meaninglessness. This is not within the power of any leader to command, but within the capacity of many thousands to demonstrate. The future flows from the alchemy of silicon, flesh, and spirit that is manifested in the lives of people who commit to doing the next right thing within their grasp.

From the highest level of government down to county health departments and school boards, the question returns to the faith groups—churches, mosques, and temples. Sometimes the request is transparently manipulative and predictable, as in almost every scheme to shift the burden for the poor from the government. Sometimes the request is merely wistful, hoping for something more powerful than money and self-interest to emerge. Jim Wallis, reflecting on this powerful confluence pushes beyond old-fashioned categories of "left and right," "conservative and liberal," toward new ways of talking about faith, morality, and social responsibilities that don't have widely acceptable vocabulary yet.[19]

The situation has anomalies. People who have not been in a congregation in twenty years now describe with confidence how churches can take care of the homeless or mentally ill. Clergy who have never been in a welfare office or juvenile detention facility are just as inexplicably confident in their ability to tell government workers how they could do a better job of dealing with juvenile criminals, welfare mothers, and pregnant school children.

Only rarely are the capacity and role of the religious structure examined thoughtfully, taking into account the radical changes in their social and technical context and how they connect to each other and to other social structures. As Loren Mead reminds us,

> God's call is to newness for the whole world, not just the church. Those of us who are called into the church have a special vocation to work for the renewal and refreshment of the church, not as an institution out of the rest, but as a centering presence from which we serve the new world that God is creating around us.[20]

Congregations Re-Envisioned

This book explores a way to re-vision the congregation so that leaders inside and outside religious structures can understand how they might be part of the process of building healthy communities. We need a new understanding of how faith groups are integral to communities, not separate; how their strengths integrate with those of other institutions to weave the roots of community for health.

To many, the congregation is the weakest link in the religious chain, the institution most resistant to change, the least obvious place in which to look for the future. Brooks Hays's definition of a church committee hangs as a warning: "the unwilling led by the unqualified to do the unnecessary." I quickly agree that this describes the vast majority of congregations who will continue to muddle along long after the future breaks in. Fortunately, the future of the church is not decided by majority vote. It is determined by the creative movement of God, who is constantly encouraging those who are leaning toward the future seeking a path of service and hope.

Mead argues that the church is stretched between a great vision of the past and a new vision of its future that is not yet fully formed. At the center of this new formation is a changing role of congregations— from being passive supporters of ministries primarily done by centralized agencies to being the front line. The familiar roles of laity, clergy, executive, bishop, church council, and denominational bureaucrat are in profound transition as a result. Mead speaks of being midwives for a new church. What will the new church look like?[21]

To those inside the old structures, innovation feels like weakness, and it spells the demise of comfortable patterns and privileges. Meanwhile, amid the most difficult and complicated problems a new stew of strengths is brewing. Hundreds of new structures within and alongside the old church structures are popping up. These are not "think tanks," experimenting to be clever. Innovation is simply finding the next thing that works in response to the urgent needs. The Interfaith Health Program comes across entire networks of innovative congregations every week, scattered from coast to coast and around the world. Many of these innovative groups are described on our IHP-NET website (http://www.ihpnet.org) and in our publications such as "What if Every Congregation?"[22]

What are the strengths in congregations that are relevant to shaping the communities where they serve? Finding the answers to this question is what this book is about. I want to help people within and without congregations to recognize the kind of things congregations do that mark their role in building communities of the future. When so many of the driving hopes and fears of our time are large scale—even global—phenomena, it may seem odd to focus on the congregation. But faith is formed in social groups where one can see it, describe it, hold it accountable, train for it, and link to it, even when the subject of faith has global implications.

Of course, not all of this remains at the congregational level. The faith community in the United States is large, complex, diverse, and fluid. Congregational life is only one aspect of the complex ways in which faith, spirituality, and religious practice engage the future. All aspects of religious practice are affected by mutating social technology that broadens the menu of how we connect to and influence one another. Denominations, interfaith coalitions, religious agencies, and secular organizations that remain influenced by religious values are all part of the larger picture. We have convened meetings at the Carter Center of more than a hundred key decision-makers from religious hospitals and related organizations. One indication of the scale of the structures is that within the next ten years it is likely that half the religious hospitals in the United States may be sold or merged, creating a flow of assets in the range of 25 billion dollars forcing religious decision makers to deal not only with their hopes, but their raw financial power. This shift of assets would be the largest transfer of assets in the history of the Church and it is only one aspect of the scale of change underway.[23]

Even within hierarchical religious structures such as the Roman Catholic or the United Methodist Church, experience at the congregational level is driving the future. In times past religious leaders had the power to command compliance of local units with larger jurisdictions. Loren Mead argues that the demands of local ministry are the driving force behind both the demise of our customary connectional structures and the rise of new ones. Not only are denominations changing their connectional structures, but local congregations are finding their energies nurtured by entirely different connections to different groups.[24] Some of these groups may be new alignments of traditional partners, while some may be new connections with government, professional groups, or other religious groups focused on specific issues though a plethora of new organization types arising to seize opportunities or confront problems.

Active and Inert Congregations

The most dramatic social innovation is happening in a small minority of congregations where the heavy lifting is taking place on the complex mix of problems and opportunities. In any given community about 10 percent of the congregations do almost all the significant community work on almost every visible issue—homelessness, battered women, violence, food, health services, and so on—and the same minority of congregations are on the founding committees. I suspect this has always been true, even in less turbulent times.

It is hard to explain the other 90 percent. I think of them as the inert ingredients that make up 98.1 percent of the contents of a fertilizer bag. Even these congregations off the cutting edge still play an important role in providing their members a context in which to orient their lives and mark their significant passages. I remember rolling my mother in her wheelchair into the back of the sanctuary across from her nursing home. She could hear only the faint outlines of the spoken words and could not participate in any aspect of ministry. But the organ played and she moved her lips to the music that had reminded her for eight decades that this was her Father's world. She was connected to her core identity and to the God who held her future—no small gift to receive.

Although I am primarily interested in strengths, it would be disingenuous to ignore the fact that many congregations are nearly toxic. (It would be impossible to overlook them, because the worst seem to be televised!) Mental health workers know that religion can disorient and obscure reality just as easily as it can be a solid foundation. Families with members who are wounded, disabled, unusual in any way can tell chilling stories of how congregations deepened wounds rather than healing them, further isolated the hurting at just the time they most needed a human face on God's grace. While not ignoring these congregations, neither do I think they are significant windows on the future, for dysfunctional forms give way over time to those that channel life.

When looking for clues to the future, we look for groups of people who are approaching the hardest problems expectantly, eager for innovative opportunities. Ironically, congregations that do open themselves hopefully are guaranteed to attract a constant deluge of problems, requests, and questions that demand new words and partners. These are the congregations on the turbulent growing edge. And reflected in their life, as in a mirror darkly, you can catch a sense of the future God is creating.

What Is a Congregation? What Is a Community?

This is not a book of theology, but it deals with organizations—congregations—that live on the boundary between human and holy. There are two temptations in trying to talk about the intersection of God and humanity in such real-life structures.

The first temptation is to simplify the intersection by ignoring the religious nuances. This approach rounds the phenomena down to mechanical, rational interest-seeking behavior that economists and bureaucrats can understand—things that can be seen and counted. Once the mystery is stripped away, it is possible to talk about the congregation as just another social structure and about religious language as the noise covering the real machinery. This temptation is frequently enshrined as basic policy in governmental organizations, at least until they try to enlist religious organizations as partners in various social and health schemes. At this point, it is easy to turn toward the second temptation, which tries to enlist the power of spirituality without the messiness of human religious structures. Granted, it is a mystery unto itself how anything spiritual can happen in a structure so tangled as a congregation, much less amid the complex bureaucratic forms such as denominations. But this is what we have to work with on this planet.

The second temptation is the opposite: to talk about spirituality as if it could be separate from religion and religious structures—in effect, to reduce the phenomena to only things that *cannot* be seen and counted. This, too, avoids the complexity and ambiguity of the social context of human search for meaning. The issue focuses on the means of expression that humans use to communicate and share their attempts to push beyond animal existence toward more ultimate meaning. With the arguable exception of music and the arts, humans have no way to higher ground except through language and structures that can at best be rough "clay pots," to use the apostle Paul's term. There is no way past the awkward tools of human interaction directly to the spiritual realm. Maybe a few of us can do so, maybe at rare times in our lives. But how would the rest of us know about it, if the spiritual athletes had not found a way back through language?

New Roles for Religious Congregations

The link between personal, private spirituality and the many social factors that affect community life is the congregation. It functions like a community within the larger community, forming, nurturing, and challenging individuals to participate with other humans in social networks. It is like a force field affecting other larger and smaller fields; it is dynamic, fluid, changeable, in motion. Thus, it not only links, but feeds the people and systems it touches. Of course, not all the influence is in one direction and not all is positive. A World Council of Churches group meeting in Johannesburg on the challenge of forming a global community built on "costly obedience" noted that at the congregational level, liturgy and practice can form and "malform" people and communities.[25]

Much is written today about the role of spirituality on a private level, nurtured apart from the inconvenience of community. Witness the growing section of "soul" books in bookstores. And, indeed, one of the most lively areas of research in the health sciences is the exploration of links between physical, mental, and spiritual phenomena. If these links did not exist, it would be hard to take faith and religious practice seriously as factors in shaping the future of communities. But while one would expect faith to be valuable at the personal level, that is not primarily where it is formed. For the most part, we learn of faith through others, hopefully by what we experience in our families, but often as adults, from others whom we trust or admire because of what we see happening in their lives. Faith can be *nurtured* in solitude, but it is rarely *born* in isolation. It is relational, something that emerges between people as they speak to their own human experience of seeking the Wholly Other, the Ground of Being—God, the ultimate presence to whom we seek to relate. The group in which that search is most commonly experienced is the congregation.

Why bother describing a congregation at all? Why not just let them go on and be happy for what they do? Gandhi said that we tend to become that which we think we already are. In the case of congregations, if we know what to look for, what to ask for, what to expect, it is likely that is what we will grow toward.

We face the problem physicists have in describing light: It is both *particle*—in the case of a congregation, usually a building—and it is *energy*—in this case a field of relationships. The physicality of the congregation—its building—frequently outlasts any of its leaders. The sanctuary reminds of times and experiences in a way that goes beyond mere photographs or written words. The congregation is among the community landmarks least likely to move around. This means that it is easy for people to find, whether they need food, counseling, prayer, or day care. It is in the physical world. But not that only.

Learning from the physicists who increasingly describe phenomena as "fields," a congregation is a social field to which people find themselves drawn and sometimes held in relationship to others and to a sense of reverence and possibility—faith. The congregation is a field of influence, formed voluntarily, that enhances its capacity to shape behavior and nurture meaning. It is a field of activity in which we try out our faith in the presence of others both similar and diverse. It is a field of coherence that awkwardly finds its way into language, rituals, and practices that help mark its boundaries, entry points, and exits.

A congregation is a field that can bring into coherence more than one relationship at a time, making other identities—husband, sister, child, citizen, carpenter, physician—meaningful in a larger field of meaning. It is a field that evokes and makes coherent new connections. A congregation is not only a physical point of connection, but a field of coherence in which new implications and applications of meaning can be found. Most importantly, the congregation is a field in which we can sense the relationship between God and God's creation.

The practical implication of thinking of congregations as fields is to realize that any of the structures that happen to be visible at any given time are temporary. It is easy to value the buildings, the spreadsheets, and the activities because they are visible and touchable. But the underlying strengths of congregations are more enduring and dependable, especially amid times of great change.

We can learn from other phenomena that endure. I was recently in the Bay area of California, where I walked among the redwoods in the Muir National Forest. These may be the only forests that can compete with the live oaks of the Georgia coast for grace and mystery. I had walked among them before, but I had never really seen them. That afternoon I found myself standing in the middle of a forty-foot circle of redwood trees, each of which was ten to thirteen feet in diameter. Even bending back, I couldn't see the tops of them. So I lay down on the soft ground, and then I could see that the circle of trees converged almost out of sight up in the fog. They were touching each other—as if they were one tree.

The most important thing to understand about a redwood tree—and about a community—is how it passes life on. Where does the next generation come from? Redwood trees don't usually spring from individual seeds; they spring from the roots of older trees. I was lying in the middle of what had once been an ancient giant of a redwood tree. The trees surrounding that circle were, in fact, the young ones. They reached 250 feet into the air, but they were the children. And they had sprung up from the roots of that mother tree where I was lying. I realized that it is nonsense to describe one redwood tree. Not only are they tangled together at the top, they are inseparable at the bottom, where their roots are deeply woven together.

Something like that is true in communities, for we, too, spring from the roots of those who precede us. We are not held up by living soil like trees, but we are sustained by the coherence, the living meaning, that we experience in our communities. That is a spiritual function entrusted not just to a few great leaders but to all of us who resonate, who believe in God by whatever name we know God, by whatever way we know God.

It would not be so terribly important to know how communities replicate if we lived for three hundred years; there would be time to get it right. But since we live only seventy or eighty years, it becomes critical to understand how we pass on that which holds a community together.

The role of congregations in weaving the roots of community cannot be dumbed down to mechanical tasks and to-do lists, for this is sacred ground on which we move with humility and a sense of awe. But we can move out in confidence in the spirit articulated by Margaret Wheatley:

> I haven't stopped wanting someone, somewhere to return with the right answers. But I know now that my hopes are old, based on a different universe. In this new world, you and I make it up as we go along, not because we lack expertise or planning skills, but because that is the nature of reality. Reality changes shape and meaning because of our activity. And it is constantly new. We are required to be there, as active participants. It can't happen without us and nobody can do it for us.[26]

In the most practical way possible, this life-giving task finds expression in the eight strengths of congregations that help build communities in the twenty-first century. Congregations accompany, convene, and connect. They give sanctuary and context. They bless, pray, and persist. These are the strengths around which our structures will form and reform. These are the channels along which we can expect to find God breaking into our midst and nurturing our communities toward life.

CHAPTER 2
STRENGTH TO ACCOMPANY

İT WAS JUST A BUSINESS CARD ON THE TABLE next to my mother's bed, but I could recognize the Methodist logo from across the room, the one with the flame wrapping the cross. I didn't recognize the name, but that didn't matter. Fulfilling the most basic expectation of the congregation, the pastor had come by to see Mom, say a brief prayer, and leave a church bulletin. She had spent a lifetime on the other end of such visits in other cities, even working for a while as the coordinator of visitation at our Methodist church back in Baltimore. I remember how she would pick me up from school, then stop by three or four homes on the way back to ours. The suburbs were quickly sprawling across former fields, and the visitation teams followed just behind the pavers. I had no idea then why we were visiting, what difference it made, or who noticed; it was just something the church did. Still today one of the basic strengths of congregations is to accompany, to be present physically, eye to eye.

Life Is "Being With"

Congregations exist not only on paper, in cyberspace, or even in their own buildings. The church is not a meeting place; it is the people scattered and gathered even two at a time. Moreover, faith is not something to "have," only an identity, a body of ideas to agree with, a brand of worship. It is more accurate to speak of being "of a faith" that moves us toward a sense of belonging, of participating in ways that are not exhausted by words or even rituals. My mom is still of the faith even though she can't get to the church building or hear the sermons or songs. It even hurts her to read much, so she is unable to read Scripture or discuss it in groups as she did for decades. In fact, she can barely hear it when read aloud, picking up mostly the rhythm and accents of familiar verses. But she is still quite literally and physically part of a congregation—they come to her. They accompany her.

For any one person, accompaniment means life itself in many dimensions, even amid frailty. It does not "fix things," but it allows for continued connection, coherence, context in which meaning and value are still possible. For a community, accompaniment also means life, the most tangible way that we are held up by and connected to others. These connections don't just happen in community; they are the essence of community. With all the focus on services and infrastructure, it is easy to miss this most obvious fact of community. One could say that a community is a group that accompanies its members through the many interwoven processes and passages of life. Most of us are part of more than one community in this sense, hopefully at least one defined geographically, but others defined by other links. Perhaps it is accurate to say that our community is the group that we have a reasonable expectation will accompany us through our various passages.

Wendy Lustbader closes her book *Counting on Kindness* with a paragraph that gets to the heart of the issue:

> The expectation that we will be able to count on kindness during our time of need becomes one of life's most sustaining convictions. We hope that if we become incapacitated, our friends and relatives will stand by us. We hope that their help will arise out of affection rather than out of pity, and that we will bear our difficulties gracefully enough to keep on inspiring their loyalty. We suspect that the measure of good life is how we are treated at the end.[27]

I suspect that the measure of a community is how we and those we

love expect to be treated during the times of incapacity that we will surely experience. Will I be accompanied at all? Will I be surrounded only by
those I can pay as long I have the money or insurance to pay them? Will
I be alone when I have no power to compel others to help me? Will those
I love be alone when I cannot care for them or protect them?

Dislocation and Isolation

The congregation works to build community over against the particularly modern experience of isolation. Life expectancy has risen rapidly throughout the twentieth century; we generally live almost half
again as long—nearly eighty years—as family members might have
expected at the turn of the century when life expectancy was only
forty-six years for men, two years longer for women.[28] Women still
tend to outlive men by nearly eight years.[29] In addition, smaller, more
mobile and scattered families make it less likely that elders will share
the family home for any significant period. On the other hand, the
vast majority of people over sixty-five are themselves far more mobile
and social than stereotypes assume. It is not until people are in their
eighties that a large number of them find themselves generally limited
in terms of mobility.[30] Moreover, more than 40 percent of those suffering with long-term disabling disease or injury are younger than
sixty years of age.[31] HIV and other chronic diseases, including injuries
and the previously unrecognized prevalence of mental illness affect a
significant fraction of our community. Often overlooked is the isolation of those giving care to the ill. Frequently, caregiving is provided
by a very small circle of family members who experience an isolation
almost as profound as that of the one who is sick.

Chronic disease and injury are not the only reasons people find
themselves on the inaccessible and invisible margins of our community.
Poverty, the loss of a job, divorce, family crisis, or any number of things
can cut one off from customary patterns of work and relationship. Our
increasingly fluid economy frequently cracks like an earthquake fault
under seemingly solid ground, shaking our economic foundation with
no warning. Stephanie Coontz, in *The Way We Never Were*, describes

the vulnerability of the nuclear family over against the rabid individualism of our time.

> Only the family, it seems, stands between individuals and the total irre-
> sponsibility of the workplace, the market, the political arena and the
> mass media. But the family is less and less able to "just say no" to the
> pressures that emanate from all these sources, or even to cushion their
> impact on its members. . . . But very few people can sustain values at a
> personal level when they are continually contradicted at work, at the
> store, in the government, and on television.[32]

Caught in the storm not of our making, we tend to turn inward to
protect ourselves and our own, fearing to give away time or resources in
the community that we may need to hoard closely at home.

And it is not only negative trends that disorient us. Positive factors
also give us demographics never before experienced by any generation. We are living much longer, and most of our added years are in
good health. But frequently we find ourselves isolated, in unforeseeable and seemingly incoherent social situations. The major causes of
disability are no longer infections or traditional "medical" problems.
On a global basis mental health, interpersonal violence, and unin-
tended injury trail only tobacco as the leading causes of lost years of
healthy life. Although gross average measures such as life expectancy
continue to move in a positive direction, there is an increasing gap
between those in favored groups and those on the margins. Economic trends magnify the differences between the well connected and
those who lack privileges. These privileges tend to be allocated along
traditional lines of gender, race, and ethnic groups. But some who
thought themselves to be safely among the favored now find that their
traditional status is only as enduring as their ability to pay their
insurance policy premiums, which they may lose due to declining
skills, age, or health. Many of us have neither economic or social certainty and find ourselves facing large-scale social changes by ourselves.
Coontz stresses that increasing numbers of groups may find themselves fractured and discarded. Exploring the dynamics of the black
family in America, she notes that

Black Americans are at the cutting edge of a number of changes in our society—some negative, some positive. Far from being the "last of the migrants," they are first of the postindustrial discards. They have borne the brunt of the restructuring of the American economy and the two-decades-long war against working people's living standards and employment security. Even though African Americans have taken the highest proportion of casualties, they are merely the frontline troops. All low-income and working class Americans, of every ethnic group, are involved in this battle; few are likely to escape unscathed, whatever their family tradition of values.[33]

Coontz draws the link between our economic disorientation and our isolation:

The crisis of the family in late-twentieth-century America is in many ways a larger crisis of social reproduction: a major upheaval in the way we produce, reproduce, and distribute goods, services, power, economic rewards, and social roles, including those of class and gender. The collapse of social interdependence and community obligation in America challenges us to rethink our attitudes toward the periods of dependence that characterize the life of every human being, young or old, in or out of the family.[34]

Coontz argues that the changed family systems and the resulting isolation call us forward toward communities and intermediary social structures, such as congregations, that surround and support families. In effect, communities that survive are those that find new ways to accompany their members through the tumultuous changes.

Ken Dychtwalk, author of *Age Wave*,[5] writes in a quite different tone about the opportunity to nurture patterns of support and relationship that take advantage of extended age, more robust medical therapies, and personal wellness disciplines. He argues that we should organize ourselves against many of the current patterns of isolation not just because they are bad for those who are frail but because they are unhealthy for every age and condition of person.[35] Nobody is healthy living alone, even if all of his or her physical necessities are provided.

Congregations Can Create Relationships

Where do religious communities fit in all this tumult? What is the role of the congregation in building communities in which it is safe to be fully human?

The power to bring people into meaningful relationships in the context of God's love is at the root of every congregational strengths. A congregation that finds ways to love each other will have no boundaries for that love. If of God, it will overflow into the community onto anyone who needs the love or anything that can be delivered through love, be it food, assistance, or simply accompaniment. This power to accompany is not a limited resource unless it is conserved and turned inward, like trying to store up wind by putting it in a bottle.

We live in a time between times when social patterns of community are reforming. On one hand, the changes seem too large and fundamental to be engaged at all. But the breaking down of old patterns also creates space for new kinds of association. The congregation is at the center of social innovation because its reflex is to come together, to seek out and include, to accompany. When so much blows us apart, the breaking down of old patterns is the key to forming new ways of binding together. This binding together does not begin in the large and public arena, but comes from the most humble and unremarkable kinds of engagement, the visit to my mother's room, the prayer group that meets for each other on Thursday mornings before work, the phone call after dinner every night to an elderly neighbor. It is around such practices that patterns solidify and grow like crystals on a string.

The congregation is a relational stew of such encounters that constantly experiment with what might be called the "relational technologies" that can help us be present to each other. In this sense, sidewalks, cars, phones, and e-mail are all tools that permit people to be accessible to each other. Phones enable us to reach out from anywhere and include another in our lives. Electronic mail permits the formation of new kinds of presence, accessibility, and even intimacy that augment other kinds of relating in ways we are just barely beginning to understand. Of course, some technologies drive us apart and push those who are weak and less-skilled to the margins. Most technologies cut both ways and depend on being appropriately adapted by social structures such as congregations. For instance, cars encourage us to scatter too widely and privately, yet they also enable us to come to each other across miles and miles if we choose. And congregations can organize car pools and visitation teams to include those who may not be able to drive.

Other relational technologies give voice to those formerly in silence to engage communities for themselves. Betty Thompson a woman with cerebral palsy, has been a member of Oakhurst for many years. We are used to her sitting near the back left-hand corner of the sanctuary. Only three years ago did she become able to speak publicly to us by means of a computer-assisted speech augmentation device attached to her wheelchair. I still chill to think of the first time she led us in corporate prayer, the computerized voice cutting away the space between us, letting us see God through her lens of experience as she prayed for us and with us.

I thought of Betty when I was with Mom one day, watching her struggle through a thicket of physical problems that made speech frustrating and slow. I turned to the Internet discussion group IHP-NET, which links together hundreds of colleagues around the world. I described Mom's situation and asked if there were any tools that might help her communicate. I learned about professional groups with a variety of devices designed to bridge the gaps that form between people as a result of disease, injury, and disability. With wonder I explored this new world of inclusion only to be reminded by Mom that our technology has far outrun our social patterns: "I don't have anyone to talk to; why do I need that box?"

If the only mediator between the individual and global possibilities is economics, the only ones who are included are those who have money. The congregation believes in a different mediator and thus can explore different patterns of social inclusion made possible by whatever relational technologies are at hand. At first fragile and experimental, the congregation has the strength to bring included people into connection with other parts of the community. If Betty can now lead the congregation of *believers* in prayer, why can't she speak to the city commission about the needs of other *citizens* like herself? Once we experience the possibility of participation, it quickly becomes normal. "Of course, Betty should do the prayer." Because she is disabled? No; because she has developed a resilient, wise spirituality previously inaccessible to most of us.

God's economy is a household economy in which the family is expansive and inclusive. Living out that reality is not abstract—it spreads like roots through the social soil from person to person, gradually creating patterns of relationship that are strong enough to support the community against heavy wind, strong enough to crack rock.

Expansive Community

At first we respond to individuals, but then—as I learned through my mom—the individual is a type, one of thousands. The congregation's strength is recognizing individuals in their particularity, but the congregation also has the capacity to form around patterns of need. For instance, a particular opportunity to visit an individual in jail gradually results in the formation of a jail visitation committee as members meet other inmates and become familiar with their needs. A member with HIV calls out a group that gradually becomes organized for long-term, not sporadic assistance; a family with a Down's syndrome son gradually awakens the attention of the congregation toward the opportunity to create a group home for him and others like him. Through the lens of particular relationships, the congregation gradually sees others, some in the church, some not, with similar needs for inclusion. Others with special needs, ostracized or stigmatized elsewhere, see that they might be recognized as humans in this particular congregation. With the possibility of welcome, they come and add to the sensitivity of the congregation, building their capacity to see, understand, and be present to a fuller range of the human community.

To those isolated by illness, mistakes, or economics the community can feel like it is surrounded by a high wall. At the Carter Center we frequently hear of prisoners and other individuals suffering human rights violations. They are isolated and hidden away behind physical and social walls. In the United States single black men in prison are about as alone and vulnerable as it is possible to be. Often they are able to find some help by moving across a slender religious connection—an individual who knows a church member, who talks to his or her pastor, who knows to call the NAACP with its strong clergy network, who can send someone into the jail to accompany the prisoner, keeping him from being invisible and silent.

In a society in which everything is marketed for sale, we tend to devolve into mere consumers. A congregation builds relationships on terms quite different from market-oriented individualism. Even congregations with clear boundaries between "us" and "them" maintain those distinctions in ways that cut across other boundaries.

It will not do, however, to romanticize what happens in such encounters. Proximity does not ensure honesty or presence if one or both parties to the relationship does not trust or value the relationship. It is possible in most congregations to pass decades without uttering an honest question or heartfelt fear. It is possible to be together for decades and never ask, never listen, never care, never reach across the agreed boundaries. How does this change? Ironically, the congregation who seeks to nurture more spontaneous accompaniment trains for it and in so doing raises visible expectations.

The tendency toward humanity is frequently submerged by the dominant social patterns. Indeed, because churches have participated in and justified the larger social patterns, excluded people must find the grace to forgive the congregation. The mentally ill, the divorced, the racially different, the drug addicted, the poverty stricken, and the nonconformists, have often felt degraded or shamed by the congregation because the congregation has pushed them further to the margins. Parents of children with disabilities are especially sensitive to the toxic effect of many congregations, quickly finding that no church is better than one that further devalues their child. Jimmy Allen, the former president of the Southern Baptist Convention, tells the tragic story of how members of his family suffering with HIV were rejected from one church after another once their disease became known. The first step toward accompaniment may well be an apology, a request for forgiveness.

A personal relationship precedes the institutional process, one person conversing with another, asking in honesty, "Who are you?" "Who am I to you?" "Is there a we?" Fingers touching like the smallest tendrils of roots begin to weave together tentatively. In time a bond may form across which the lifeblood of community can flow.

Building Patterns of Accompaniment

Congregations build patterns of accompaniment in communities in at least five ways.

Including the Frail

1. *The congregation includes the frail in community by creating relational systems beyond ties of blood and money.* Being a member of a congregation establishes obligations, responsibilities, and privileges that stand alongside blood family links that may not be dependable for many modern reasons, including distance and small or broken families. Likewise, although the market is rapidly creating new forms of reimbursable assistance, few would consider such aid a dependable source of relationship. The congregation can augment both and in some cases even replace them. (This is essentially the situation recorded in Acts 2:42–47.) The congregation accompanies its members, not just because they are frail, but because they are members and have a claim on its resources. Even though my mother attended the local Methodist church near her nursing home only twice before her declining mobility prevented it, her lifelong faithfulness as a Methodist made the pastor's visit something she could legitimately expect. She was "of the faith"— not a supplicant, but a member, a believer, one of the congregation. She knew that the church visited people like her as a matter of course. That is what the visit meant and why it brought coherence and a sense of relationship. It reminded her who she was and to whom she was connected. Thus, it reminded her of her value, not her frailty.

The congregation creates, nurtures, and trains for enduring patterns of expectation of accompaniment, which Wendy Lustbader refers to as "exchanges." She observes that people with a history of generous exchanges with others tend to carry these inclinations with them to the end of their lives. "Wherever they live, whatever they do, they readily make connections with other people and derive satisfaction from doing so. When frailty encroaches, they tend to be surrounded by loyal helpers. There can be no certain formula for security, but kindness is rarely wasted and the habit of generosity almost serves as a strength."

The congregation is frequently a place where a lifetime of such "exchanges" is encouraged and experienced. When one has established such an identity, it becomes easier to accept assistance as a dignified part of being a human being. Lustbader continues:

> The belief that there will be people around to assist us during our time of need is the conviction that we create by our own example. . . . We see firsthand that individual efforts can indeed reduce suffering and that not all hardships are beyond human control.[36]

Creating Helping Roles

2. *The congregation creates helping roles that make it easier for people to voluntarily engage those who may be outside of their normal range of vision.* People who join a congregation don't just come to receive; they come with the expectation of giving, and they expect to be changed by the giving. When we organize roles that systematize accompaniment, we make those expectations more accessible and tangible. It isn't just the frail elderly who need accompaniment, although increased longevity will only multiply open doors. Opportunities exist whenever someone is in need. For example, Everett Hullum became my dearest friend when he insisted on accompanying me as I took my terminally ill dog to the veterinarian to be put to sleep. He could do nothing for the dog, but he knew that I did not need to be alone, so he took a day off from work to be with me.

Many of the large social and governmental systems seem overwhelming and inscrutable, especially to those who have any impediment of age, race, education, finances, or ethnic background that adds to the sense of estrangement. The congregation can keep track of those members qualified to accompany others through various systems and offices, help with paperwork, and answer questions that might other-wise mystify and isolate. Today there are few more isolated people than the families of prisoners. Increasingly, prisons are located in remote rural towns far from urban centers or public transportation. In Georgia a small group of congregations working together as the "Friends of Prison Families" organizes transportation to prisons for family mem-bers, housing and feeding them overnight at congregations near the facilities. They also offer training for family members in their legal rights, as well as counseling on how to deal helpfully with parole and, eventually, the time of release. The Sullivan Center in Atlanta is one example of hundreds across the nation that offers legal and financial training for welfare clients along with occasional food, clothing, and economic help. Government systems seem designed to be hostile and intimidating. Religious people stand with those in need, helping them negotiate what can be a humiliating and difficult path. This cannot be done with brochures and a website. It happens only when one human makes eye contact with another, accompanying them on the way.

The congregation can also be intentionally sensitive to those likely to benefit from such practical accompaniment. Such help doesn't require a computer. I remember starting a training session for health profession-als on how to evaluate the health status of their congregations and neighborhoods. It happened that we were meeting in a Sunday school classroom. Just before launching into my sophisticated presentation, I noticed the chalkboard with the handwritten prayer list. The Sunday school class had naturally brought most of the relevant health issues of which they were aware before God and their group. The prayer list then became a Monday to-do list of phone calls, rides, and visits.

Some people need special or new kinds of accompaniment. In recent years congregations everywhere have found themselves learning how to respond to people living with HIV. For most, dealing with HIV vic-tims has initiated a thicket of questions, fears, and confusion that has let to a stigma similar to that experienced by the mentally ill or criminal offenders. Many congregations have dealt terribly with the epidemic, but others have found their way forward. As the epidemic has gone on, the issues have changed, because people living with HIV are no longer dying quickly. In many cases their lives become similar to the frail elderly, and congregations good at handling short-term crises have had to organize themselves for much longer relationships.

As congregations become aware of groups of people with particular needs, they can systematically equip their members with skills to respond. These response teams do not need to be invented from scratch, because there are a number of specialized organizations that offer well-designed training for particular caregiving needs.

Building New Networks

3. *The congregation builds networks and helping systems through collaboration and through the creation of new organizations to deal with systemic needs.* The average congregation in the United States has less than four hundred people, which means that there is a limited pool of people needing specialized accompaniment at any given time. In a handful of neighboring congregations, however, there is likely to be someone with HIV, mental illness, or Alzheimer's, or who will be recovering from surgery, injury, or a difficult pregnancy, all of which demand some specialized preparation for caregiving to be more than symbolic. The Federation of Interfaith Volunteer Caregivers (FIVC) has developed hundreds of collaborative networks of congregations across the nation who share a coordinator of volunteers, ensure adequate training, and tend to administrative details. Many of the teams begin because of a member who has a specialized problem. That person opens the eyes of the congregation to larger neighborhood needs and the opportunity to share the burden and to minister to others.

Most of the FIVC networks actually create new nonprofit corporations with their participating congregations as their board of directors. Other similar kinds of extended networks build on existing collaborative, usually ecumenical, organizations. In many cities the ecumenical networks that emerged decades ago to collect and distribute food and clothing are now the hub of housing, rehabilitation, shelter, counsel, and specialized caregiving.

Changing Expectations

4. *The congregation infuses other community structures with healthy social expectations.* One would hope that any member of a healthy congregation would naturally receive any assistance or accompaniment that God would wish that person to have. The constantly shifting balance of giving and receiving should be as unremarkable (yet as life-giving) as breathing in and out. The relational patterns promoted for members within the congregation, however, are not exclusive privileges of those members but are normative for the whole community. The point is that God wants to revive all of creation. The congregation is just a demonstration plot of what God wants for the whole community. Accompaniment is not the alternative to advocacy, but the rich experiential soil from which it grows, the link between health ministry and health care reform activism.

When a congregation finds itself drawn authentically into the presence of people living with HIV, for instance, it will not just create a caring enclave; it will also engage the larger social structure to move it toward a more humane role too. Accompanying may mean going to a city commission meeting, zoning board, or Chamber of Commerce to help the full community finds its deeper humanity. Many of the people who need to be accompanied are representatives of types of people who are for one reason or another invisible or silent in the public square.

Offering Visibility

5. *The congregation makes otherwise invisible people visible to the community.* The congregational network can learn about people who might be invisible or excluded and then bring them into the public times of congregational life, especially worship. The point is not to make them a spectacle, but to make their presence and membership in the community normal. This may mean going out and picking them up, which is preceded naturally by calling them, visiting them, making them welcome, and making their surroundings comfortable and convenient for them. The worship service may run a bit more ragged when you have to walk around wheelchairs in the aisles, or when people with mental illness take up the offering, or when the choir doesn't hit every note.

When a woman in a wheelchair leads the congregational prayer, it may take a minute or two of fumbling with the microphone because she has to pray from her chair on the floor rather than from the pulpit.

For those outside the congregation it is important to understand that accompaniment is not only a service but the crucial means by which the congregation learns. They see people, not patterns. They then see patterns through the eyes of the people they accompany. The congregation's other powers to connect, convene, give sanctuary, and frame messages are unlikely to express themselves until members form personal relationships with people who need those things. Government organizations are frequently moved quite differently—by data from large-scale analyses. Most congregations will be unmoved by appeals based on data until they know somebody affected and, through accompanying that person, come to understand how they can help. Thus a government welfare office seeking to engage the strengths of congregations in the community will do so by asking one of the congregations to accompany one or two clients and form ongoing relationships with them.

Once a relationship has been established, it is possible for congregations to hear the data, see the pattern, visualize the group, and mobilize their other strengths to respond in ways that may be more creative and radical than previously dreamed.

CHAPTER 3
STRENGTH TO CONVENE

T HEY CAME TO THE CORNER, AS THEY HAD FOR thirty-two years
from back when Compton was a suburb, not the epicenter of violence. It was youth Sunday at New Mount Calvary Baptist Church, an
in-your-face affirmation that guns and drugs did not have the last say,
that hope was stronger than fear. The kids had the choir loft on this
day, and it was already vibrating with drums and electric guitar as the
guest preacher followed Rev. Lonnie Dawson to the podium. They
slipped into the red velvet chairs as the kids in the choir slipped into a
higher gear, finding their voice and rhythm.

Sol Alinsky warned that one should never go up against a group
that sings together. But in fact, many forces went up against these kids
every day. Every kid in the choir knew friends who had been killed by
gunfire, and most had been threatened themselves. The city in which
they grew struggled to pay its teachers, health workers, and police.
The poor and rich were breaking apart like icebergs from a rapidly
warming glacier. Each kid knew the dark side of life at the end of the
twentieth century; the fear, the lowered ceiling of aspiration, the fierce
undertow that pulled each toward deep, cold water. They knew what
it was to walk home afraid and to have their fears confirmed. But in
this place they also knew what it was to walk in hope and have that

confirmed too. It was no small thing for them to sing about the power of God.

An African-American worship service usually involves nearly everyone in the room in one way or another. The preacher is often misunderstood as a performer. Actually, he is more like a director, making sure that every voice in the congregation finds its place. On that Sunday we came forward to bring offerings, to ask for special prayers by the deacons, and again for announcements. We—the preachers, teachers, police, factory workers, nurses, bus drivers, shop owners, clerks, grandmothers, students, homeless, old, sick, and well—were brought together.

Convening to Find God and Each Other

The most basic strength of congregations is that they congregate, or convene. From the time of cave paintings to the day of the Crystal Cathedral, people have come together to find God. Today, basic techniques of relating to one another are changing. How we come together; how we learn of and from each other; how we listen, speak, support, and gather are changing.

People of faith expect God to be able to draw us together even when so much pushes us apart. This doesn't happen magically, but through the mundane technologies in congregational offices. Look what God has to work with in most congregations: computers, copy machines, directories, phones, mailing lists, and meeting rooms. The church is no longer part of the "command structure" in society. Nobody *has* to come when the church calls or do what the mosque says. But amid the decline of many other unifying social structures, it can convene. It has the capacity to bring people together across lines that frequently divide; such as profession, economics, race, and self-interest.

Many of our community problems result from failure to implement creative answers we know about. It is almost impossible to compel people to think creatively, much less to take a risk based on a creative thought. Imagination is evoked, called out; it reflects a hope for the future. It cannot be forced or compelled or commanded. It flourishes when diverse people are brought together in hopes of finding a way forward. Thus, the most powerful possible action is to convene, to draw people together.

The power to convene is easily misunderstood by those outside the religious structure. Even though they know that modern people show little respect for governmental or academic authority, they may think that the church, at least, retains the power to tell people how to behave. This is not true. So how does a congregation convene when it can no longer command? The congregation does not now play the stereotypical role of setting forth and commanding allegiance to a set of behavioral norms. Some wish that it did. Such stereotypes fit the wishes of government and corporate interests who feel increasingly powerless to compel behaviors they think best. In fact, I suspect that the role of the church in creating, much less enforcing, such norms has almost always been overstated. Rather, theological language is like the glove on this fist of practices designed for the convenience of economic systems, be they feudal, industrial, or today's postindustrial forms. We see that the religious glove is easily adapted to ethnic divisions and the oppression of minorities.

Today we function in an economic system in which many people and their inconvenient relationships are unneeded by the productive systems. The social debris of drugs and suicide, the families that break apart, those who are malformed and those who never form, the youth with no future, and the cities abandoned by their suburbs are by-products of a system that simply doesn't need certain entire categories of people. Those benefiting from the changes want those on the margins to be quiet, to acquiesce, and perhaps even to be tended by somebody else. Maybe the church could command patient acquiescence? And it would be even better if religious groups could be persuaded to provide food, shelter, succor, and health services too.

Anyone who has ever served on a church committee knows that congregations do not have the authority to command or the raw power to provide a sustained flow of goods and services. Their power to convene needs to be understood in the context of the loss of all institutions to command obedience in modern society. The question moves from whether faith-based groups can command collaboration better than others, to whether they are more effective at nurturing voluntary actions in the right direction. The first critical test is the capacity to convene.

Dr. Nancy Ammerman argues for a continuing role of congregations in forming healthy communities because of, not in spite of, the fact that they are voluntary associations. She notes that the overall population of congregations in the United States is at least stable, if not growing. The religious sector as a whole exhibits "remarkable vitality" which flies in the face of a long tradition of sociological theorizing. Louis Wirth Toennies writing in 1938 contrasted urban and rural forms of social life with urban life being impersonal, superficial, transitory, and segmental. It was axiomatic that in the cities family, neighborhood, and church would lose their binding and ordering influence.

Even when religion has continued within modern life, it has been assumed to be one segment of many activities, "occupying a small niche in the complicated lives of urban persons and communities." The other alternative was to relegate faith to "an internal, individual meaning system." Actually, the history of community disintegration in the United States is far more complex—and the role of the congregation as a counterforce equally complex. Congregational strengths described in this book are not based on the traditional roles defined by a social ecology that no longer exists except in imagination. They reflect a still-emerging role in modern society that is shaped by humans working together out of shared meanings voluntarily chosen.

Just because more of us live in cities does not mean that we live with fewer and more distant relationships. It does mean that most of these relationships are chosen from a large menu of options. Congregations are voluntary associations, which amplifies, not diminishes, their significance. For the same reason that especially difficult or perilous military tasks are assigned to volunteers, congregations are more capable today because they are purely voluntary in nature. People are there for many reasons, but among them is the hope of being transformed and nurtured so that we might amplify our individual efforts to shape the world for ourselves and those we love. People are in congregations on purpose and that purpose makes all the difference.

Congregations convene for many reasons: worship, discussion, argument, service, teaching and learning, planning and organizing, celebrating and grieving. They serve as a lens that focuses and concentrates social energy that otherwise would remain diffuse and incoherent. Even a catastrophe like the death of children by gunfire, for instance, can fail to mobilize action unless the grief is focused. But even when anxiety pervades a community, a congregation can convene an astonishing range of people—a previously impossible feat—to see through the fog of fear and incoherence.

Convening in the War Zone

Violence is a good example of the process and consequences of convening strength, for it seduces us to substitute fear for hope in every contact with those outside an increasingly narrow tribe of people. The prevalence of violence in our everyday thinking and experience sets a shrinking boundary on every hope for a humane, sustainable, just future. Every night television says, "Lock your doors and fear everyone outside your tribe. Do not expect anything but death from a stranger. There is no reality but fear, no god but someone on your side with a bigger or quicker gun. How could you think otherwise?"

Firearm homicide does not begin with violence against women and the young, but it includes them as particularly accessible victims. By 1992 in seven states firearm homicide was the leading cause of death for all youth between ages ten and nineteen. The Centers for Disease Control predict that this will be true in all states within a few years as firearms eclipse auto accidents. The ages of both victims and perpetrators has continued to drop.[37]

Violence, especially handgun violence, is a hemorrhage in the community, literally draining away the very lifeblood that sustains us. While it certainly reflects the failures of the past, even more certainly it foretells a failed future marked by tribal antagonism and uncreative attempts to dominate and coerce. Humans from more "primitive" times would probably be amazed at the scale of violence in the United States. How could our ancestors understand that having conquered smallpox, polio, and dozens of other plagues, we are powerless to protect our children from handguns? Which of us could explain why penicillin requires a prescription while a nine-millimeter pistol does not? Could our forebears have imagined that the twenty-first century would be launched in a hail of gunfire in the streets, making violence the leading cause of death in urban centers?

If we expect to go up against this grim cadence, we had better come prepared for a long, creative struggle. Part of the disease of violence is a preoccupation with quick fixes. Humans are not machines; they create incredibly complex and tangled networks of problems. We are not going to solve the problem of violence anytime soon and will only compound it by approaching it with images of blaming and forcefulness similar to its own.

Violence is rooted in tribalism—the reflex to fear those who are different, to define as "us" a smaller and smaller circle of people. This happens not just in Africa and Bosnia, but in tribal America, with its white tribes and urban tribes marked by color and deprivation.

Because tribalism lays at the root of violence, the first step toward peace is to move closer toward those who are different from us in language, religion, wealth, education, color, and nationality. As long as we ask about violence while surrounded by people just like ourselves, we will see no further than our own image. We must move beyond the division of "us" and "them" or "them" and "others." In one way or another, as long as our question is rooted in our tribal identity, we will always be asking, "How do we protect *ourselves?*" We will seek to rationalize our patterns of privilege. We will justify the inevitable pattern of control, punishment, and—when it fails, as it surely will—retribution.

In a practical Monday-morning way, we must learn to recognize as an ally anyone or any group working for peace, tolerance, justice, and dialogue across boundaries. None of us can wrap his or her one life around all of violence. We need to see the links, to begin to break the problems into response-able pieces. This is impossible to do in the abstract; somebody needs to convene a meeting.

For example, in 1994 the Carter Center brought together thirty experts on youth firearm injury to see if there were interventions that offered the hope of success in reversing the terrible tide of death among our kids. We tried to be rational, approaching the cruel crisis as we would a public health outbreak. Facing over 5,000 teen deaths in 1991, could we hope to reduce the number by half in five years? We recoiled at the thought: What kind of a twisted goal is that? Perhaps, then, we would be bolder and try for 90 percent reduction. Even that defies sanity. Who could imagine telling hundreds of mothers that their sons were within the boundaries of expected and acceptable deaths?[38]

The answer—the only answer—was that not one death was acceptable. Not even one. This proclamation became the moral floor on which we could stand as parents, brothers, daughters, and neighbors to seek the way out. The moral clarity of "not even one" opened our eyes to the many tasks that needed to be done.

We knew youth firearm deaths were one expression of a cycle of violence. We needed a way to get inside that cycle, to understand the root causes of the deaths and to find the intervention points to prevent the cycle from occurring with other kids. We decided that we could at least look at every death and try to learn where the community missed its chance with that young life. Every life is worth at least understanding what happened. The police ask who was guilty. We want to know something different: We want to know where we missed the chance to prevent this death so that we may prevent the next one.

We convened small meetings of community people and national experts and found a remarkable similarity of perspective that crossed barriers of age, race, education, and life situation. Nobody can reconstruct a life, or a death, within the boundaries of one discipline. It takes people from the faith community, the schools, law enforcement, and community organizations, as well as some age peers and some people skilled in public health investigations. Together, looking at one person's life and death, an interdisciplinary team could begin to see where the cycle of violence could be broken in very specific ways. But who could convene such a group on the streets? Congregations can.

A teacher in Atlanta took our early plans and turned them into action when a young student in her band class was killed while walking near the school. Antonio was killed close by a rapid rail station while walking a path through a poorly lit and overgrown lot. Emily Campbell mourned, but she wiped the tears to ask "Why?" She gathered a team from the community, built around Antonio's fellow school band members. They began looking at where he was killed, investigating why the lighting was bad, why the lot was allowed to be overgrown, and what other violence had happened there—always asking what the community could do to prevent another death. The police are still working on convicting Antonio's killer, but already the community has found some practical ways to act. Some will demand new laws concerning the cheap handguns favored by the small-time junkie who ambushed Antonio to steal seventy-five cents. Others only demand an afternoon and a lawn mower to clean up lots where kids cut through on their way to and from school.

The Role of the Faith Community

Is there a special role for the faith community in such a violent time? Although worshiping groups have no special technical expertise beyond the police or schools or various health agencies, the house of worship can be a safe place to ask questions with tenacity and honesty. If we can say that we do not have all of the answers, perhaps other experts will do the same and we can begin to learn from each other. Faithful people cannot solve violence by themselves in our pluralistic, multicultural world, but they can be the catalyst toward a strategy that weaves the community together.

A convener that moves from humility, not power, opens the doors to a host of potential collaborators. When the Carter Center began to map the movement against youth firearm death, we found a plethora of governmental, religious, voluntary, business, union, and civic organizations eager to work against the violence. Prophetic voices like the Children's Defense Fund are joining traditional institutions such as the YMCA and almost any civic group with a conscience. At local levels these groups often find it awkward or difficult to collaborate in sustained ways. They need a safe space in which to gather and a moral framework bigger than their own self-interest. A church, synagogue, or mosque can be that space and provide that framework—if it does so in humility.

It is true that violence is taking an increasing number of young lives every year. It is also true that literally thousands of congregations are rising to the call, opening their eyes to the violence and their arms to the violated.

Martin Luther King Jr. bet his life on the ultimate weakness of violence.

> [Violence] is a descending spiral, begetting the very thing it seeks to destroy. Instead of diminishing evil, it multiplies it. . . . Returning violence for violence multiplies violence, adding deeper darkness to a night already devoid of stars. Darkness cannot drive out darkness; only light can do that. Hate cannot drive out hate; only love can do that.[39]

We might prefer our hope to flow from certain knowledge, especially that which we can footnote and prove. It will not be that way with violence, for fear will always demand more data than is available before we risk anything. Knowledge follows—refines—hope. This does not mean that we move in darkness or in isolation from the tough realities. For while our century has been filled with blood, it is ending with a truly astonishing array of congregations and organizations committed to following the God of peace.

New Mount Calvary Baptist Church is one such church. The congregation is the anchor of the Not Even One campaign in Los Angeles, the driving force behind a large-scale "keep it good in the hood" campaign, and countless other efforts to engage the despair in the streets.

This is no witness from the fringe. In congregations like New Mount Calvary, the police, teachers, social workers, and the whole web of the community find the memory and the hope that are stronger than all that seeks to tear their lives apart. The songs and prayers are personally powerful, but the public and social experience of hopefulness is what binds the transformation in place. The social web woven in the congregation stays in place as the people take the hope with them the next day to their places of work and learning. The kids, cops, teachers, and preachers all know that violence does not have to win.

Congregations in every city show us that violence is not like gravity, binding us down into the inevitable dirt. In every time and place, God opens a path toward peace and reconciliation for those who seek it. It is not a path away from violence, but one that leads directly into the heart of our broken times, into the lives of broken people.

Congregations like New Mount Calvary are able to convene not because they stand apart and above the community but because they are totally enmeshed in it. As Ammerman notes, "congregations are linked to other parts of the community through the multiple memberships and loyalties of their own members. But they are also linked as organizations to larger organizational networks . . . with more access and power than they might have on their own."

The capacity to convene is anything but abstract. And what happens in worship is only the smallest fraction of the story. The office of New Mount Calvary tells the story even better than the sanctuary. It is constantly swamped by a dense rain of information concerning every conceivable problem and hopeful initiative for miles around. Indeed, a glance at the mailbox shows a deluge of information from around the world. The copier rarely stops running, and boxes of leaflets are stacked near every wall. The phones only stop ringing when one of the secretaries or volunteers is making outbound calls.

Rev. Lonnie Dawson's Rolodex, which is filled with all sorts of information, is hard to find on his desk but it is the envy of politicians and organizers all over the country. Dawson's phone list is not just made up of "contacts" but of relationships formed over decades of meetings, burials, marriages, births, and personal passages. So when Rev. Dawson calls a meeting about violence, his invitations are considered and respected. Others may have more sophisticated phone systems and more cybergadgets; the church, however, has just enough mechanical tools to get the word out with the credibility to be heard.

Convening depends both on developing credible relationships and on refining the technologies for those people to intersect. Again Ammerman understands: "The overlapping of concern and leadership makes the boundaries between congregation and community quite permeable. The social ties formed in the congregation are essential links in the community infrastructure."

As New Mount Calvary demonstrates, the meeting doesn't have to actually take place on church property. It can pool its convening capacity with other faith groups in ecumenical and interfaith coalitions of different sorts. And it can lend its authority to secular and professional associations. This is not a blank check, however. The convening capacity is not a command authority, but is dependent on its humility and hope. When that humility is co-opted by self-serving political interests in the service of the powerful, it quickly finds that nobody will come when it calls except those who seek their own interests.

Tending and Mending the Web

How does a congregation nurture its capacity to convene? It is tightly integrated with the other eight strengths, of course. The greatest asset any congregation has is the complex lives of its members. Even young members have multiple interests, affiliations, relationships, capacities, and responsibilities. Most people add to their complexity with each passing year. The lawyer is also a soccer coach, works out at the YMCA, has clients all over town, has children at three schools where he participates on PTA committees, and has a mother in a nursing home. His former wife is a social worker, and his current wife is a nurse at the community hospital. Before law school he almost went into the ministry and still thinks of going to seminary and working for some community ministry. Older members have rich webs of relationships, most of which are invisible because they may not involve the exchange of money or goods.

The strength to convene is not owned by the professional clergy. It lives within the complex and interwoven web of multifaceted relationships that constantly change over time in the congregation. No database can be sophisticated enough to capture or organize the flexible power of such relationships. The image of the network, with echoes of wires and computers, is far too simplistic. Karen Papachado, the mayor pro tem of Aiken, South Carolina, likes the image of the spider web, which must be tended and amended every morning. "In human community, you have to work the web of relationships all the time." People are never the same, so the networks constantly change whether we realize it or not. This shifting complexity can be unnerving for those who want to draw clean organization charts and get everyone in the proper place. The power is in complexity, not precision.

People are convened across relationships by a human being whom they regard as credible. Most real issues in communities have multiple facets that demand the attention and commitment of people from many sectors and backgrounds. Nobody knows everybody; nobody has credibility with all sectors. The congregation is a rich pool of relationships that multiply the potential reach and credibility of any invitation. The most practical way to prepare to convene is to constantly stir the relational stew at every possible congregational gathering. The more the members know about each other, the more likely it is that they can help convene or be convened. Some old fashioned techniques and some new technologies can nurture this strength.

1. *Keep your contact list accurate and up to date.* Addresses of current and former members, as well as of key people on the edges of the congregation, are basic. Make it easy for people to find each other using all methods of contact. Postal addresses are good, phone numbers better. What about fax numbers, e-mail, and beepers?

2. *Tell stories about meetings large and small that model the power of convening.* Mention such stories in sermons, and make time for them in worship or over dinner. Hold up as heroes members who successfully gathered diverse groups around difficult issues.

3. *Think small and particular.* The most significant convening often involves small, carefully chosen intensive groups of people who may or may not know each other. It is hard to imagine any mechanical system that can keep track of the full complexity of any real group of humans, much less of the multiple potentials that complexity could link with community issues. The human brain is well-evolved

to handle such links, especially when filled with God's faith and compassion.

4. Focus the convening through personalized mail or, better, phone contact. This ability builds on the relational credibility of the congregation. Simple computers are all the technology you need for this communication. Voice messaging systems are only a small step higher in sophistication. E-mail contact is increasingly powerful but not yet universal enough to be dependable across age, sex, and economic barriers. Even now, however, among subgroups of teachers and professionals, e-mail is a high-impact tool for convening.

5. Go to great lengths to understand the multiple connections to other organizations and interests your members represent. It is tempting to want to computerize this step, but humans are so complicated that such a technology would not be useful. Most churches are small enough to keep track more directly. Allow plenty of time at worship services, dinners, and retreats to stir the relational stew.

6. Strengthen the capacity of laypeople to be conveners. Pastoral leaders can do this by coaching this strength among official leadership, such as deacons and elders. And they can encourage laypeople who hold prominent roles in their professional or working careers to function as conveners by developing the faith-oriented characteristics of humility and hope.

As in other key strengths, practice builds capacity. If a church develops trust in wide sectors of the community as a place that is safe for controversy and serious about seeking answers to common problems, people will seek it out, asking for it to play to its basic strength, the capacity to convene.

7. Do not focus primarily on one-time, high-visibility, crisis-oriented convening. Rather, there is great potential in small, ongoing groups convened around more enduring questions. For nearly two years on the first Monday of each month a small group of pastoral counselors met with us at the Carter Center to talk about the profound changes in the health services marketplace that were edging them to the sidelines. Gradually, trust grew, and we were able to share our individual plans and our weaknesses. We pushed into questions that were not safe, for which we did not yet have answers. The counselors found the will to risk joint actions that would have been impossible only a year before.

8. *Instead, convene around questions rather than answers.* Realistically, once an answer has become articulated, it will likely take on the tint of one discipline or another. Unless the answer emerged from a diverse and trusting group it will have little capacity to generate risk among a broad group, even if promoted by enthusiastic people of faith. But when a trusted person convenes a group around an honest question, willing and eager for full insight, they are at their greatest strength.

The fruit of convening depends on the exercise of the other strengths of congregations, as well as on the inherent gifts that lie with the other people and groups who come together. Convening is a basic strength a community looks to from a congregation because it is the key to catalyzing the other resources that might otherwise remain out of sight and reach behind boundaries that divide us from one another.

CHAPTER 4
STRENGTH TO CONNECT

I T'S JUST ON THE OTHER SIDE OF THE RAPID RAIL STATION from the Doraville General Motors plant. Thousands of people drive by every day on their way to work at the plant or to catch the train to downtown Atlanta thirteen miles away. Probably the only ones who notice the brick church are looking hard for some help and know to search for the ministry center. They go to the side driveway, find a small sign, and head up the stairs to a clean, wide-open room with three desks. Here is the underwhelming hub of a plethora of connections in the community. Sam Bandela is the master weaver who connects things and people: used carpet to bare floor, food to empty stomachs, illegal immigrant to bilingual lawyer, lonely kid to Vietnamese Bible school, scared mom to women's shelter. More importantly, he weaves people: those in need to those who have; those who need to serve to those who can use some help.

Disconnected Communities

Chamblee-Doraville is like a small Los Angeles in its rapidly shifting ethnic diversity. Only a few years ago a small white footnote to the map of metro Atlanta, the town high school now has kids speaking more than thirty languages. All varieties of Hispanic and Asian groups have settled here, some clinging for survival while others build blocks of restaurants, stores, and, of course, churches. This is a town under deconstruction and reconstruction at the same time. The disconnected pieces are scattered around the streets like my daughter's box of puzzles. Kathryn likes to dump all her puzzles on the floor, mixing the pieces into an impossible clutter. She knows where the pieces go and can put them into place, but nobody in Chamblee knows quite yet where all the pieces of their social puzzle go.

The little brick church demonstrates the third basic strength of congregations, the power to connect. While the power to convene focuses on bringing people together, connecting is marked by creating links across which resources, assets, power, and knowledge flow throughout the community. Sometimes, as is the case with the Chamblee-Doraville ministry center, the connections mature into whole new organizations that become part of the community's organizational infrastructure. When this happens, it is easy to forget where the organization came from, how the meaning and purpose were formed, where the leadership was raised up and challenged—in the congregations. Once these connections become visible and tangible, they are easy to name. They are what people like to call "social capital," a limited resource to be invested carefully in the highest community priorities. In our time when nothing is valued until it has a price, naming something "capital" is supposed to be an honor. Actually, in business, capital is a secondary asset, with the primary one being creativity, knowledge, imagination. Even on Wall Street, capital is just money until somebody has an idea. If you want to build a community, you don't start with social capital either. For a social infrastructure is just a skeleton until it has compassion and discernment. These are what breathe life into the connections, and they depend on the strength of congregations to nurture them.

Deep Connectedness

The connections that give life don't just sit and wait; they move. They themselves are alive because they are human. They move because they are on their way to somewhere new that doesn't quite exist yet. More accurately, they would argue that it lives in the mind of God and in the faith of those who follow God. Far from resisting the future, they feel beckoned by God toward opportunities.

The skeleton of the faith and health movement in communities is comprised of the collaborative structures that connect organizations. The movement is mostly made up of many separate organizations that are held together by external, often ad hoc, structures. We will never find a common home in which everyone is comfortable. We don't need it. The skeleton locally, and at every level of community, is a connectional structure that permits us to learn from and to work with one another.

This model of connecting assumes that we are different and will remain so. It does not expect to find a uniform vocabulary or single faith. It does not assume that we will naturally drift together. It assumes the opposite, knowing from painful history that it is more natural to distrust and fear, more natural to drift apart into ever-defensive small circles of us and ours. It seeks a deeper connectedness that is not tripped up in mechanical linkages and trendy vocabulary.

For most of this century Christian churches have been trying to negotiate their way beyond the embarrassing and redundant multiplicity of denominations and jurisdictions. Entire forests have disappeared to make the paper for all the conference publications. Some old sources of dissension have been solved; but new issues have emerged to divide again. So it is in relationships among different faith groups—Jews, Christians, Muslims, and others. Communities cannot wait for the discussions to end. And they are not. What we find is that long before systematic analysis congeals and negotiated unity emerges, communities can move together around problems and opportunities if people are nurtured in their faith to look for God amid the emerging connections. They sense that God is there in the stew and move toward it hopefully, not away from it fearfully.

This has a mystical tone that may obscure the fact that the current move toward collaboration is so clear-sighted about human communities that it seems almost cold-blooded. I stress this because it is easy to be mistaken for a fool when one is working seriously for the future. Only a fool believes that any one denomination, any one science, any one governmental agency has the power, resources, or insight to bring healing to the community. Only a fool would say, "Follow me, I have the answer," or perhaps only a fool would follow. Rather, we move toward one another in humility, challenged by the opportunity for making progress and needing one another in order to see progress achieved.

Faith Risks Trust

The cornerstone of any collaboration is respect for the integrity of the component partners. This is especially true in the area of interfaith health, because the movement finds common cause among groups that do not have a common worldview. This is not a matter of manners and civility. Again, if you want to work together in community, you had better respect the integrity of your co-laborer. This is where collaboration usually breaks down, because it takes time to respect someone. Cultivating respect for someone different from you, someone operating out of a different faith tradition or scientific perspective, takes time. You cannot respect something you do not understand. You cannot understand someone to whom you have not listened. You cannot listen to someone with whom you have not spent time.

It can be somewhat threatening for a Christian to find common ground with a Muslim or Jew or for a public health scientist to explore the religious role in healing and prevention. In general, collaboration depends on people comfortable enough in their own worldview that they do not fear differences. The congregation is the place where such risk-taking faith is formed and reinforced.

The point is, the movement of faith and health will support, not eclipse, the underlying religious structures. It depends on strong, coherent, and confident congregations who understand their own tradition and are capable of challenging their members to act on central ethical claims for health. A congregation that sounds and acts just like a public health agency is not very useful to the public. A public health agency that tries to sound and act like a church is not very useful to the faith community.

It is easy for utilitarian collaborations to run roughshod over the worldview of others and damage the source of enduring community connection. This happens when houses of worship are viewed as mere delivery points for health interventions or, conversely, when public health agencies are viewed as mere funding agents to support church programs. A little perspective could help here. If a religious tradition has survived for 3,000 years, it deserves credit for its insight into how the world works. On the other hand, for 2,900 of those years we were generally satisfied with a life expectancy of less than 50 years. Public health science deserves most of the credit for extending that to 75 years in the last century. Maybe health scientists know something too.

Two Principles of Collaboration

Respecting a partner is actualized in two street-level corollaries: respect for the survival logic of the partner and limited domain collaboration. Collaboration can be quite difficult because organizational survival is often difficult. For ten years I ran a small nonprofit organization that rarely had more than a couple of months financial reserve. Although I believed in collaboration then as strongly as I do now, in many cases I had little room to maneuver. My first responsibility, as is every direc-tor's, was the survival of the organization for which I was responsible. Smart collaborators begin with a tough-minded understanding of the organizational needs of their partners, in particular, money and atten-tion—which lead to political and volunteer support.

The survival logic of different organizations may be quite different from one to another. Simply asking, "What does your organization need out of this collaboration in order for you to enthusiastically par-ticipate?" will go a long way. Don't assume you that know what someone else needs.

The second practical corollary to respecting the integrity of your partners is what I call limited domain collaboration. Formal collaboration is difficult and time-consuming and can be threatening, so don't overdo it. There is something about an incomplete coalition that drives its leaders crazy. In many cases the coalition never actually does anything substantial because it is always waiting for one more critical component to join. "We'll be ready when the police participate; we'll take that risk when the chamber is on board." Limited domain collaboration is comfortable with incomplete connections, ready to move on the basis of what it already connects.

My model for limited domain collaboration is the Tucson Care Fair, where Silver Darner and Rebecca Melland-Buckley quietly built a coalition of normally contentious and defensive agencies from every part of the community. Once a year they come together to offer free service with no hassle to anyone in need.

They do this with little money and the most limited ongoing structure. The agencies participate because the rules are clear and the commitment limited. The Monday after the fair, everyone goes back to their normal contentious habits, but they go back slightly changed after seeing what is possible when the interests of clients are put first.

Limited domain collaboration is especially important in dealing with religious organizations, because they are overwhelmingly volunteer-driven. Successful collaborations do not attempt to win the heart of the collaborators, but remain as temporary conduits for their common goals. The heart of the movement is provided by religious traditions trying to live up to the best of their faith. The heart remains in the congregations and other faith-forming entities. In effect, the congregations are the heart that pumps the blood of life into the skeleton and flesh of the community.

Where is the brain of the movement? The movement of faith and health in any community reflects a convergence of scientific analysis and faith. Applying all that we know of preventive techniques and community policy could result in extended life spans, and extended years of active, productive life. Freed from preventable diseases and supported by healthier life choices and wise environmental policies, we can imagine a far greater experience of the abundance God intends of human community. This is a vision worth working for, one that can call out our very best labor.

Five Gaps to Bridge

As we will see in later chapters, the discernment depends not on creating some elite committee of smart people, but on a network of diverse relationships that is pervaded by a spirit of hopeful but honest inquiry. Congregations can build their connections with purpose and intelligence. In our work with groups around the country, we have found that discernment explores five kinds of gaps, each of which can be approached systematically.

The five gaps lay out the kinds of knowledge that inform what a congregation needs to know—or at least ask—as it follows God into the community. The only way to know is to ask, engage, connect. Peter Drucker, in *Post-Capitalist Society*, explains that

> Knowledge is not impersonal, like money. Knowledge does not reside in a book, a databank, a software program; they contain only information. Knowledge is always embodied in a person; carried by a person; created, augmented or improved by a person; applied by a person; taught and passed on by a person; used or misused by a person. The shift to the knowledge society, therefore puts the person in the center.[40]

Drucker is dealing with what shapes society in a time when the traditional drivers of economic and social change—land, capital, and labor—are increasingly secondary to knowledge. This knowledge dynamic is at the heart of the congregations' changing role and power in shaping communities, for it focuses not on static assets and services, but on the capacity of the congregation to be a space in which human connections are nurtured and sustained.

Learning—accumulating knowledge—is not a step that precedes in the old-fashioned sense that school used to precede work. Neither is ethical reflection a separate middle step between knowledge and action.

The strength to connect is built on the willingness to reach out to others, to other institutions, with partial knowledge that learns *in the connecting*, more fully what God may intend for the community and therefore what we must do.

The *first gap* is to look for knowledge that is accepted but not applied. Almost everyone has a list of such ideas within his or her own area of expertise. Specialists in preventive medicine are decades in front of hospitals and governments in terms of knowing how to prevent disease and injury. Imagine what would happen if the leaders of churches attended their meetings and immediately examined their programs to apply the best knowledge.

The *second gap* is the distance between commitments we have already made and what we actually do. We frequently fail to realize that old commitments are relevant to new opportunities or problems. Changing technologies constantly shift the menu of the possible, opening options for good or bad. Some demand careful examination by ethicists, but most are more mundane and tangible. Most congregations are decades behind science in terms of implementing the most basic public health perspective in their communities. Why? One reason is that they have not remembered that at the core of the ethical tradition the prevention of suffering has always had a higher priority than after-the-fact caregiving. Before immunization, sanitation, and food inspection were developed, the ancient commitment toward prevention was not as relevant, because disease and injury appeared to be capricious. But now we know how to prevent most of what was once regarded as unpredictable and unavoidable, so our commitments to prevent suffering are suddenly highly relevant. A leader's task is much easier when the focus is on reminding a group of something they are already committed to as opposed to convincing them to take on a brand new idea without roots in their tradition. The second gap assumes that faith groups have relevant commitments to their communities that can be uncovered and dusted off, and in doing so find them life.

The *third gap* lies between the projects that are successful and the many other places where they could be applied or adapted. You don't have to reinvent Habitat for Humanity; you can just do it or adapt it. Neither do you start from a blank pad when engaging prenatal nutrition, caregiving for HIV victims, support for substance abusers, legislative abuse of the poor, famine due to drought, youth homicide, or elder abuse. There are programs already well developed whose success can be adapted quickly in your own situation. Frequently, you can invite somebody from a relevant project to meet with your group and shorten your learning curve dramatically by telling you their experience, with its serendipity and plan. Any project changes when it is rooted in a different community and led by different people, so you can expect it to evolve in your own environment.

The *fourth gap* lies between your current relationships and the many potential partners with whom you do not presently work or learn. The most important kind of knowledge is found in new relationships. Most of us are limited by the fact that many of our colleagues look and think just like we do. This is the gap that makes the first three nearly intractable, for how could I know about problems or opportunities that come into focus only through different eyes. How would I hear of new techniques from other fields, reflect on my ethical commitments, or recognize new models of action? Sometimes this is the stuff of surprise, but it can be just as systematically developed as any other body of knowledge. This knowledge is usually not found in libraries but over coffee. And it isn't magic; you have to pick up the phone and call somebody.

The *fifth gap* is a little harder to understand, especially for action-oriented Americans: the gap between our current deeds and future needs. What are the long-term implications of today's choices or omissions? This is not something that can be known with certainty. But even asking the question brings a new level of awareness and creativity to the search for the right thing to do. Dr. William Foege led the successful global effort against smallpox—the first time in history that the world cooperated actually to eliminate a disease. He points out that when you hold an infant today, you may be in the presence of a citizen of the twenty-second century. So our horizon of concern should extend at least that far. But many of our choices will have ramifications long beyond then, so we should place our decisions in a different context.

A Symbol for the Movement

What is the symbol of the health and faith movement? We could think of great symbols: something like the Million Man March, or the immunization needle, maybe a scientist with a test tube, or a preacher at a pulpit. I suggest that it is a committee meeting, the most despised tool for change we have. I learned this from my father, who died a couple of years ago. I have reflected on his eighty-six years to find their meaning and unity. He believed in the church, the community, and his country. He wasn't much of an orator, and only very late in his life was he elected to public office, but he was a great member of church, community and government committees. I learned from him that your values will show through the committee meetings you attend.

All this science and theology boil down to finding the collaborative tools that allow us to come together and do the right things for health. It is so simple but so difficult that we must learn from each other and encourage each other. How do you confront HIV and violence, hunger and tuberculosis, mental illness and the politics of greed and privilege? You form a committee and get to work.

Healthy Connections

Sometimes congregations develop new organizations that remain within the structure of the church or synagogue. One of the most interesting is the family of initiatives known as "parish nurses" or, more generically, as health ministers or health promoters. The classic model was developed by Dr. Granger Westburg who brought a doctor and nurse into a congregation so they could promote holistic health, including medical care, preventive education, counseling, and pastoral care.[41] Over the years the model has mutated toward a more affordable model that depends on a nurse with special training in the congregation. Hundreds of congregations now have some professional health staff, frequently linked to and partly paid by, a hospital affiliated with a religious group. Perhaps as many as 6,000 congregations have other mutations of the idea, usually depending on volunteer medical professionals in the congregation, sometimes acting as a committee of volunteers.

The health promoters of the Chamblee-Doraville churches are laypeople from many professions nominated by their congregations to receive special training. The Carter Center and the Ministry Center connected the congregations to the Emory School of Nursing, which conducted training in health promotion and basic prevention skills in response to the needs identified by the lay health promoters. St. Joseph's Hospital, a Catholic institution, assigned two trained parish nurses to support the lay health promoters, and the Dekalb County Health Department also made available staff to help connect the congregations to other government resources.

Because the health ministers come from health professions, they tend to describe their work in medical language, but they rarely provide medical treatment of any kind. What they really do is connect, using health language as a lens to bring the needs and opportunities of the community into focus so that the appropriate connections can be recognized. Without the nurse, the congregation may see only hunger, depression, disability, aggression, homelessness, unemployment, violence, and injury. With a trained health ministry, the congregation sees problems for which answers exist if connections can be made. Most of these problems are not only individual failures, but symptoms of a broken web of relationships that keep people from getting appropriate assistance and, as importantly, keep resource-rich agencies from those they are designed to help. So health ministers spend most of their time connecting people, agencies, and the congregation in all its complexity.

Health ministers connect people systematically, intentionally. They weave the web of relationships, associations, structures, and individuals to build the community. If a healthy community is a fabric, the health ministers are like the needle to the thread, guiding it back and forth, here and there, tying it into a whole.

Avoiding Disabling Connections

John McKnight warns us to avoid creating structures that concentrate on "fixing people" who are labeled in terms of some disability or another. He points to family members who "almost always have a vision for the labeled individual that reaches beyond access to community services. They see that the good life is not just a fully serviced life, but one filled with the care, power and continuity that comes from being part of a community."[42] He has studied what he calls "community guides." People "do not just introduce one person to another; they bring a person into the web of associational life that can act as a powerful force in that person's life." Guides see more than deficiency. They have a "special eye for the gift, the smile, the capacity of those who are said to be 'in special need.' Focusing on these strengths, they introduce people into community life."[43] In essence, they connect people, based on their strengths, into the community. How does a guide do this?

McKnight points to three characteristics of guides beyond their ability to see strength where others see only deficiency. Guides are rooted in multiple associations in their community, which means "they know people who know people." Second, they work from trust, not institutional authority: "If guides are well connected, it is because they are trusted. And that trust is the result of having invested their lives and commitments in the lives of others in the informal web of associational life." He tells of a guide who introduced—connected—a person to a choir director. "I'm a friend of your sister Mary, and she said that I should ask you about the choir you direct. I have a friend who loves to sing and has a beautiful voice, and I think that you might like to have her in your choir." Finally, McKnight notes that guides "believe strongly that the community is a reservoir of hospitality that is waiting to be offered. . . . The belief in a hospitable community is a critical ingredient in the work of successful guides. . . . They are enthusiastically presenting the gift of one to the hospitality of the other."[44] Connecting people into the web of community does not deplete the resources of the web, but the reverse. Every thread woven into the fabric strengthens it, makes its capacity more obvious and accessible to others.

Connecting to Advocacy

Sometimes the needs overwhelm the resources, as most expect to happen as recent federal social-service budget cuts finally bite at the local level. The congregation, precisely because it is the locus of a thick web of connections, can speak with authority about how and by whom the damage was done. Connectedness is tightly linked to advocacy, public witness, and even protest.

The call for justice is merely noise in the political system unless it comes from those who are connected to the problem with compassion and intelligence. A committee based in a congregation that has demonstrated by its actions that it cares and understands the problem has considerable standing in the political arena. A politician can see that a congregation that can produce volunteers to connect with the poor can probably produce voters and volunteers that can connect for or against candidates too.

When the pastors of the collaborating congregations of the Chamblee-Doraville Center met to discuss the growing edge of health ministries, it was natural for the Hispanic pastor to ask for help in picketing the Georgia legislature to bring attention to the dangerous implications of changes in immigration laws. Since they were connected, they understood.

How Does a Congregation Develop the Capacity to Connect?

Map the existing connections. An eye-opening exercise for a congregational retreat is to cover a large wall with paper and try to draw a map of the linkages that already exist. You might use solid lines for official links such as denominational relationships or local ecumenical organizations and dotted lines for more ad hoc relationships. Draw in important links such as the flow of donations or special offerings and the help of volunteers. Use different colors to indicate special issues or concerns: youth, elders, environment, peace making, evangelism, schools, food. Leave plenty of room for the congregation itself. You might want to show the points of connection within the congregation—to the youth group, deacons, elders, Sunday school classes, pastor, and so on—or just to the building.

Is the map cluttered with relationships that are no longer meaningful? Are important concerns unconnected? Do members participate in organizations that have no connection to the congregation (perhaps environmental groups or other causes)? Are some parts of the congregational structure totally inward-looking, missing chances to be a livelier part of the whole community? Are most of the connections to groups of the same economic and racial identity as the congregation?

The map probably reveals some missing connections and provide an opportunity to convene people around the issues. Perhaps a member who is interested in a certain issue could be sent as a scout on behalf of the congregation to visit potential collaborating organizations. This can be a great way to enhance the responsibilities of the membership.

Look for Patterns of Need

Although personal stories are the lifeblood of congregational awareness, institutional connections should be driven by consciously looking for patterns of need. Public agencies, sociologists, or researchers can be extremely helpful in identifying the patterns of need that are hidden behind the power of individual anecdotes. What is the pattern of teen pregnancy, substance abuse, homelessness, immigration, tobacco use, or intentional injury in our neighborhood? How are these patterns likely to change in response to larger social patterns underway? These are questions that are unlikely to emerge from a stream of personal stories and experiences, even if the stories are accurate. The patterns of need should illuminate strategic connections and should be intentionally developed. Who could refuse having coffee with a pastor and lay leader who, as a result of an analysis of public health data, want to establish a relationship with the leader of the state refugee office or local welfare department, for instance?

Some people seem to have a gift for making such connections.

Identify the "natural connectors" in the congregation and recognize their gift as another gift of the Spirit as significant as the gifts of any other in the arsenal of faith. A natural connector is a person who always seems to know somebody in just the right organization needed for the task at hand. The connector thinks in terms of people but is also aware of the institutional roles. They don't say, "We need to contact the welfare office," but "Let's give Jim at the welfare office a call and see if he can make something happen." Someone has said that any of us is only seven phone calls away from anyone on earth. Natural connectors know the first couple of phone calls to make.

Some congregations assign members to attend school board, city commission, and zoning board meetings. This trains potential connectors and raises the visibility of their role in congregational life. The list of significant structures that should at least be monitored might include Rotary meetings, neighborhood groups, political party events, and "cause groups," such as environmental, peace, or hunger organizations. They should be encouraged to identify themselves by congregational affiliation, to make clear that they are listening for the congregation and will report back on possible opportunities to connect.

The information that flows across the web of connections creates the kind of problem a living congregation wants: too many concerns, opportunities, questions, issues, answers, hopes, people, needs, and resources to keep under control. There will never be time for all the announcements, meetings, and urgent conversations! This is the whole point, of course—to nurture more of the ragged connected life.

CHAPTER 5
STRENGTH TO TELL STORIES

It is not enough for a movement to have logic or justice or even millions of people on its side; it has to be able to tell powerful stories about how the society has changed in the past and how it could change in the future.
—Fred Block, *Trumpet Notes*

Two questions constantly confound leaders in government, business, and non-profit groups: why do people continually make choices that go against the best data and advice? And why do people so frequently choose against the best future for themselves and those that depend on them? We are deeply confused about the linkage between knowledge and choice. This is increasingly problematic because most people experience greater and greater freedom of choice. As we saw earlier, the most significant health risks are no longer infectious diseases, but those risks that flow directly from the choices we make for ourselves and those that depend on us. In our modern times we are awash in data, information, expert advice. New communications technologies make it easy for almost any of us to find technical answers quickly. What we are missing is the larger story in which we can understand ourselves. Until we know the context, we cannot know what to do with ourselves, much less the knowledge we have. Who has the power to give individuals, neighborhoods, and communities stories that can be trusted to guide us? The challenge of where to find unifying, trustworthy stories confronts business, government, and leaders of all kinds as they are discovering that it is quite literally true that where there is no vision, the people perish.

Many peer into the future wondering which powerful kind of organization will provide the unifying stories around which our communities will find their meaning. The fact is that the faith communities, including Christian, Jewish, Muslim, Buddhist, provide powerful, energizing narratives that have demonstrated the capacity to guide societies through times of profound change many times in the last several thousand years. Stories of exodus, crucifixion, salvation, repentance, mercy, jubilee, covenant, denial, journey, and faithfulness have proven capable many times before and are by far the most likely to be trusted again in our current wilderness of meaning. Religious people have frequently treated this powerful language as an internal proprietary language or as a tool for domination. The stories are so powerful they can easily be abused by false prophets (themselves prominent and recurrent characters in the story-line in all scripture!) However, the strength to story, handled with humility, can be for our communities like cold water in the desert (another good story).

The Atlanta Interfaith AIDS Network includes more than a hundred congregations that help one another develop caring ministries for people living with HIV and AIDS. The network provides training for individual congregations who desire to create care teams and facilities offering day care and pastoral support. The network is run by volunteers from participating churches and synagogues. Because of its frontline role with HIV victims and their families, the network is also frequently called on by journalists and professional and clergy groups. Participating congregations have earned the authority to tell the story of AIDS in the context of a larger story of faith, compassion, and community.

To Tell the Story Is to Frame the Meaning

Much of what a congregation does on any particular day is tell stories that help people understand the connection between events and relationships. A congregation not only tells stories, but acts them out and offers roles for its members and others in the community to play out. The congregation puts things in context by telling and reinforcing stories that explain who we are and how we should act. It does this not only for individuals, but for families, communities, and social movements.

The relationship between reality and narrative leads us into very deep water. Dr. Dick Hester is a pastoral counselor in North Carolina who helps congregations and nonprofit organizations discover their underlying strengths. He contends that the key is to uncover their often untold strong narrative from their problem-filled story. He likes to tell the story of three umpires who were talking about their profession. The first one says, "There are balls and there are strikes, and I call 'em the way they are." The second says, "There are balls and there are strikes, and I call 'em the way I see 'em." The third one says, "There are balls and there are strikes, and they ain't nothin' until I call 'em." We have grown jaded today and no longer trust that the stories we hear in the press are "the way things are." Indeed, perhaps the link is the other way around: The stories create the reality—at least all the reality we can comprehend and respond to. Congregations are often looked to by politicians and secular agencies for assistance in delivering specific messages about preferred behaviors, and they frequently do so. But they have a much deeper strength, which must be explored: the capacity to make the meaning that gives messages a context.

Some issues are clearly profound. What does it mean that my son has HIV? What is the relationship between God and my partner's Alzheimer's disease? Why do I have prostate cancer? Why did Mark's car have to hit that tree?

Some issues are remarkably unremarkable. The significance is that there seems to be no reason to challenge the way they are commonly understood. A child killed by a friend playing with their parent's handgun is obviously "accidental." What confounds the grief is that the story of the death usually treats it as a capricious, unforeseeable event that was all but unavoidable, when it is actually quite the opposite. The emotional reaction to an unforseeable event is powerlessness when the appropriate emotion might be quite different. In a similar way tobacco's role as the single most common cause of death is rarely dealt with as a story that has any religious framework, that might involve major themes of justice, sin, or greed. The story line in which the realignment of our health system is addressed treats it as a technical exercise beyond the reach of religious themes and categories, much less within the reach of dialogue within congregations.

Discerning Our Story

Stephen Carter describes three steps toward integrity: (1) discerning what is right and wrong; (2) acting on what you have discerned, even at personal cost; and (3) saying openly that you are acting on your understanding of right from wrong. A person is integral if the three are consistent.[45] The first two obviously demand time, reflection, and the nurture of courage and character. The third demands the same careful discernment, for it puts the act of integrity in context.

Putting health in context actually puts everything in context, from the intimate to the ultimate; it establishes the relationships between experience, fact, belief, hope, and fear, and also between the past, the perception of the present, and the future. What is the proper context in which to put the fact that my deacon has HIV? I have to understand something of the disease and its transmission and treatment, including the large amount that is currently unknown. I may or may not need to think about the relationship between sexual orientation and practice and religion and religious practice. I may have to think about whether the congregation should or should not publicly do anything about the disease and those living with it (and why or why not). I may or may not even want to know about the complex life, only part of which is labeled deacon: Who is this person as father, husband, lover, friend, believer, and professional, and how many of these roles are changed by the fact of HIV?

One way to frame a story is to outline the narrative, to express the underlying flow, direction, and significance. My daughter Kathryn is in the first grade as I write this. She recently asked, "Dad, what do the

Easter bunny and eggs and flowers have to do with Jesus coming back to life?" We had just finished dispensing with Santa a few months earlier, and while we had never pumped the bunny into Easter, we were discussing this at our dining room table, where (oops!) there sat a basketful of Easter eggs we had dyed together the day before. A first-grader recognizes that a lot of our activities are as insubstantial as the fake grass in an Easter basket. In effect, she was asking, "What's the story?" What parts of the Easter narrative are dependable and what is just entertainment?

A congregation reflects and reinforces an unfolding story, affirming a particular meaning of what has happened in the past that can be trusted to shape what happens in the future. What's the story of my life? What's the story of my neighborhood, my city? Humans are storytelling creatures, whose behavior individually and socially is driven less by genetic templates than by the stories we understand ourselves to be playing out. As we were trying to untangle the Easter bunny from the resurrection, we saw on the news where thirty-nine well-educated computer programmers from a San Diego suburb killed themselves acting out their part in a cosmic story that ended with them on a spaceship hidden from the rest of us by the Hale-Bopp comet. One would think that a member of such an intelligent species as human beings would have some sort of genetic boundary that would kick in about that time in the story and say, "This is a defective narrative; do not eat that poisoned applesauce." But people literally live and die by the stories that they trust to interpret their lives.

In a counseling setting much time may be spent pulling a subconscious story into the open. Frequently the plot line is filled with problems and victimization. It is no easy task to help someone find the power to rewrite his or her role toward a preferred narrative. Likewise, if unchallenged, a community's story writes its own next chapter in a recurrent plot. The miracle of South Africa revolved around the radically different stories of white and black that made armed violence seem inevitable. A different story took hold, empowered greatly by religious groups, and a different narrative was opened up for participation.

Elements of Story

To understand the power of narrative and the responsibility of the congregation in framing reality, one has to understand how much of a narrative is malleable and must be chosen or at least accepted. At the very least a storyteller must choose the following.

The cast. There are roughly six billion people on the earth. Who is in the story and who is not? For that matter, are only living people in it? What about those who precede or follow? For example, the stories that drive the violence in Serbia and Bosnia begin with betrayed ancestors. Americans, on the other hand, usually seem to have conveniently short memories. Does God play a role in the story? Are the characters people like us (and therefore establish some sense of identification and accountability) or are they fantastic figures like the Easter bunny (which have little bearing on anything at all)?

The point of view. Is the story something we witness passively, or do we actively participate in it? Is the story about "us" defined in some narrowing way over against a larger "them"? If the congregation is the narrator, it is important to know if the community is in the story as part of "us" or as "them." Is the congregation at risk in the story, with their actions having a part in shaping how it turns out? Or is it really about what will happen to others and why we don't need to care, as is the case with many morality stories about people who are different from us. The story of the shiftless and irresponsible poor says that if the poor were simply more like us, they would be OK. To share with them and change the attractiveness of our lives would be almost unethical.

The order of events. Evaluators of programs write much of their story when they choose what to measure and how to count. Few professional evaluators even try to account for religious factors in individual, much less community, health outcomes, for instance. So the story can't possibly align with faith perspectives. Likewise, choosing what phenomena to include in the stories we tell to explain teenage pregnancy is crucial: storks or sex, prayer in the schools or male predators, lack of access to birth control devices or lack of attendance at school.

The plot. What is going on? What is the moving, linking power at work? "For God so loved the world . . ." is a plot line; love is the power that relates everything. Diseases linked to tobacco cause more deaths than any other factor is a fact. But what is the plot? Does this reflect the insidious effect of rampant and callused greed (my vote). Or is it the unfortunate evidence of personal irresponsibility that goes with the human condition? (You might just as well try to avoid injuries by demonizing gravity.)

The ending. The whole point of the Christian narrative is that it isn't over yet. The first shall be last and vice versa means that all the evidence isn't in to justify a rational conclusion yet. Just wait until the end of the story. The ending point of most narratives is more immediate but still leans into the future. The story of tobacco can be told in a way that ends with the choice to smoke, or with cancer, or with a painful, expensive death, or with the costs and grief borne by those who remain after the individual's death. The ending point dramatically shapes the narrative.

The venue. The context in which the story is told is part of how it gives context to the listener. A sermon on Easter, a talk to the Lions Club, an anecdote shared over coffee, an illustration in Sunday school, a cartoon in a school paper, an op-ed in the city paper, a media event arranged for local TV, and testimony before the zoning board are all quite different settings that affect how the story is heard. Sometimes small shifts change the story. A baptism homily is different if those being baptized include young children and a recovered drug addict.

From time to time I have the privilege of conducting funerals for people estranged from a mainline faith tradition, often gay men who have been alienated from church. Last year I was asked to conduct the service for the nephew of a dear friend who was a volunteer at the Carter Center. I found myself meeting early on a Sunday morning with the man's complex family, which included three of his partners over the years, his mother, brother, and several friends. They told me stories of his life and the outrageously caring things he did to help people of all kinds. During the service I read Isaiah 58 and 1 Corinthians 13, both of which describe the kind of activist, reckless love God recognizes as faith. In the context of that man's funeral and the stories of his selflessness, those Scriptures found their context reassuring his friends of who he was.

The narrator. The storyteller is part of the story. The congregation frequently thinks of the pastor as the one with the responsibility of narrating the essential story of their life. Actually, everyone in the congregation is a storyteller. In many cases, the most appropriate and credible narrator is not the pastor, but a lay leader who is also a public health nurse or a teacher or a grandmother, because that person's full identity blends a secular credential that undergirds the authority of the story. Early in Oakhurst's engagement with people living with HIV, the chairman of our deacons was one of the lead researchers on AIDS at the Centers for Disease Control. When Jim said we needed a committee to minister to people with HIV, we listened, and it happened right away.

It is impossible to frame an event without becoming part of the frame. Thus arises the inevitable and pervasive problem that all of us and all of our institutions are flawed, imperfect frames. A story of sacrificial concern for the poor told by a wealthy, comfortable pastor becomes the reverse story. The frame—the hypocritical religious leader—turns the story into a parable about how money blinds us to our own greed; likewise, a sermon about racial brotherhood given before an all white congregation, or an invitation to attend worship extended to a person in a wheelchair when there are no ramps or elevators in the building.

A Story Is Not a Fact

Although it is powerful, a story is self-referential, perhaps only internally coherent. A story is not a fact. It does not prove anything in the scientific sense. It only offers up a coherent way of linking things to each other, which may or may not earn the trust of listeners. Does the frame of understanding explain what they need to know with a level of certainty appropriate to the risks they need to take? If so, it may become their own story, because it interprets their lives in a way they trust to guide their choices.

Sometimes a story is embedded in a symbol or a metaphor, an allusion. I once sat in a committee meeting considering a proposed initiative dealing with substance abuse prevention. The decision turned on a metaphor when someone commented that "drug abuse is the Vietnam of domestic policy." Nobody wanted to play any part in that story. How different to have said, "Drug abuse is the oppressor of our cities and 'we must overcome,' no matter what."

Are difficult community decisions like a war to be won or lost, or like a dance in which we must create patterns out of difference? In the face of changing demographics, it is possible that "we shall not be moved." Maybe we will be "pilgrim people," in that the congregation feels faithful in moving elsewhere. Or maybe it is time to see ourselves as the innkeeper in the parable of the Good Samaritan tending to those in need.

A story may or may not reflect what is actually going on in the community. Even a true story may not be relevant to the decisions that need to be made, decisions that could be informed or malformed by the power of a story that sets the frame of understanding. In fact, a true story can illustrate a false pattern, as happens constantly with stories about the poor. A preacher who doesn't look at the epidemiological data for her parish is just guessing at the relevance of the narrative she includes in her sermons. Likewise, a Sunday school teacher teaching about the Good Samaritan without talking to the local welfare office administrator about the patterns of need is unlikely to be connected to reality. A missionary who tells stories of heroic foreigners bringing help to the poor Africans may obscure the larger reality that the Africans are poor partly because they send far more money out of the country in interest payments to the banks in rich countries than they receive as charity. Maybe the relevant Bible passage to go with the story is Jesus and the money-changers, not the Good Samaritan.

Technology and Story

It is hard to talk about any aspect of knowledge or information without dealing with the changing menu of technologies, especially the Internet. Within a few years it is likely that most homes in the United States will have access to the Internet, which creates a relational channel as or more potentially significant as the telephone has become. Imagine how differently the congregation would function in connecting our community without the phone and car. Within a decade or so the Internet will likely be an integral part of how the congregation functions to weave the community. The problem is that today the companies and organizations running the wires are playing out a very different story about those being connected. A congregation sees humans woven in community; they see individual consumers—at best citizens—in a marketplace of services and data. Their plot line has almost no place for those not already privileged.

Even the most commercial of interest groups claims to be interested in how to bring about the optimum health outcomes for the largest number of people. Likewise, the shape of how communities are accessible to each other is of fundamental importance to faith groups, for it will determine how we can minister and be present to each other.

Congregations engage critical community decisions not just with a different message, but with a whole different context of meaning. For instance, congregations see the task of connecting people differently because we don't think people are just "consumers" and we do not consume health as rational individual choice makers. We are social creatures. Most obviously, the critical years for physical, emotional, and mental development are when we are too young to make many health decisions for ourselves. By age six our mental capacity and physical capacity to absorb the stresses of life are pretty much in place. And once we become mature, we still find that we tend to live and behave largely the way we were raised. We don't fully know how this works, but it is clear that rational response to data is only one (small) component. When you consider that the leading causes of death mostly result from the cumulative impact of years of small decisions, rationality may be the least weighty component. And we should not forget that our health decisions also reflect the heavy impact of encouragement from those who will gain financially from our short-term decisions. We don't just choose what to drink, eat, and smoke: we are sold.

Health isn't random. Premature death and low quality of life tend to manifest in groups quite differently based on race and economics, especially over time. People pushed to the margins of our society by race or money don't have good health outcomes for numerous reasons that compound over time, even unto their children.

What do our modern information tools have to do with actual causes of premature death? The first rule of medicine is to do no harm. Our communication strategy may violate this right from the start if it becomes just one more tool for privileged access to relative advantages that will accelerate the division between the rich and poor. Relative advantage compounds over time with dangerous health outcomes. Specific health messages rest in a frame of larger narrative about how communities are connected.

If you are sick or when someone you care for is in danger, what you really want to know is, "Who can help me? Who cares about me and my child enough to find me some food? Who can protect me from my violent neighborhood? Who will help my father stop drinking and stop hitting my mom? How can I get a ride to the doctor? Who can I count on when I am too weak to take care of myself?" Compared to these questions, real-time access to my health data is pretty small potatoes.

Health knowledge that makes any difference is knowledge that is acquired across a relationship of trust and put into action through connections with other people and organizations. The real message is communicated by weaving a sick or marginalized person back into the social web of a community that still values, respects, and loves him or her. This reconnecting is the healing function—the most powerful health information. The knowledge that somebody competent cares is healing knowledge—the rest is footnotes.

So the critical question concerning how we use the specific tools of the Internet look quite different in the context of the faith groups' narrative of the community. What if a critical plurality of congregations in any one community were trained and wired to serve as competent health knowledge gateways? It might take 30 percent of the congregations to get sufficient coverage to make a difference, maybe less. Given access to the web and staffed by trained volunteers, such congregations would be a trusted gateway into the web of health services and information. Marginalized people are going to have great problems with the technology no matter where you put the box: They will be tripped up by language, eyesight, or some other disability. But if they knew that somebody at the church or mosque down the block could help them figure out how their problem could be answered, they would probably give it a try. And, if that answer was accurate and helpful, it likely would be trusted enough to be acted on. This would be significant for the person, and also eventually be important for whoever would otherwise see their health problem at a more advanced and expensive stage. It would be a connectional strategy built on a narrative of inclusion, not consumption.

If the key community organizations—many of them likely to be religiously based—were active online, the health system would be stronger. Of course, it also would be less likely to be free to play out a story based purely on economic criteria.

It is not comfortable and easy for secular structures to engage religious organizations precisely because of the different underlying narratives about how life works. But things are not nearly as difficult in the field as it seems in the abstract, especially if both sides carefully choose their narratives to be sure they are consistent with what is actually going on in the community. Hospitals, politicians, government agencies, health departments, and faith groups know how to work with one another when they want to. And there is good reason to want to, especially if you think that the people on the margins of our society are significant.

Practical Steps toward Giving Context

1. *The first step is to become conscious of the messages the congregation is already sending and receiving.* It is usually easiest to begin with specific groups

that are especially important for one reason or another. What are you saying to elders in the neighborhood, for instance? How are you communicating to those who are not members of the congregation? Do you have a newsletter, do you visit (who, when, why?), or do you have signage they may see? Do you organize anything of special value for them? (How do you know it is of special value? Did you ask anyone?) Is your congregation accessible to them, physically welcoming? Do any of your members attend events where elders might congregate or take part in community forums where their concerns are addressed? Ask your older members to "read" the congregation's life to see what it says to them and, perhaps, to others like them in the community. You might meet with blank stares of shock that anyone wants their opinion, which may say more than their polite answers to your questions. And you may have to find a way to ask in a way they feel comfortable answering—over coffee in their living room rather than over the phone, for instance. One could do the same kind of intentional listening to many different kinds of groups in and near the congregation.

2. *Take an inventory of stories to which the congregation is listening and how they receive them.* Who do your people trust? Where do they look for stories and information that help them interpret their lives and the life of the congregation? What books and magazines do they read; what TV programs and personalities command their attention? You might be astonished to find where they are learning. What media do they have access to? How many of your congregation can receive e-mail or faxes at work or at home? You might ask what one or two specialty journals or websites they read to stay abreast of their own field, especially if you have members with specialized training in a field to which your sermons relate (health care or welfare reform, for instance).

3. *Challenge the metaphors.* Listen for the compressed stories that hide in the open in worship, prayer, hymns, and on signs around the church. You will hear all sorts of violent images describing politics, social events, and the process of change even within the congregation. The small words are often the most significant: Who is referred to as "we"? If

a task is difficult, how is it described? For example, if a congregation is trying to raise funds to replace their education building, is it "an enormous challenge" or is it "a problem." The words are clues to a whole story playing out beneath the conscious life of the congregation.

4. *Go after the commercial messages that entangle with faith.* Faith is always being co-opted by people trying to sell things. Our holidays are almost irredeemable, especially Christmas and Easter, which have come close to returning to their pagan roots. The fact is that faith institutions and vocabulary have potential to shape the values, hopes, and decisions of communities. Even though it is something like pumping out the ocean, it is worth it to keep at the task of reclaiming the faith experience from the swamp of commercialism. The most virulent and crass abuse of faith is usually found on TV, where images are crafted with such care. You might consider getting the congregation to jointly agree to ban TV during Lent or Advent one year to see what difference it makes to the experience, especially to the children. The point is to challenge the influence of commercial stories in shaping faith experience and priorities.

5. *Tell personal stories.* The Certain Trumpets Program trains progressive advocates to follow the example of the great journalist Ernie Powell who told the story of the Great Depression by his masterful use of personal anecdotes. Even when describing the role of large federal programs, he would recount a narrative with a specific farmer or small businessman. When you tell personal stories, make sure they fit reality and fit the ethic appropriate to the larger story of faith.

6. *Capture and turn events.* We humans have a problem holding a lot of information in our heads for long, so we create holidays to remind us of important events. Many of these holidays find their roots in insights that have, over time, lost their way. For instance, Mother's Day began as an antiwar mobilization in which mothers were challenged to take up their responsibility to protect their sons from nationalism and aggressive war. I don't think even Hallmark remembers that. It would make a

great opportunity for women's groups to cast off the fluff and take to the streets. Few U.S. sons now run the risk of dying in a war, but handgun homicide and suicide is a leading cause of death for young men in all parts of the country. Where are the mothers? Maybe on Mother's Day they could even get their husbands to join them.

Likewise, Valentine's Day is a nice candidate to recapture, and with it, a deeper story of what love is about. This day has been bent to fit the pleasure-seeking escapism of our culture, but its roots lie in the story of sacrificial, selfless love that even the apostle Paul would like. In fact, why not reclaim 1 Corinthians 13 while we are at it? I had the opportunity to do that this year, when I was with a group of people taking Shalom Zone training in South Carolina early in the morning, the day after Valentine's Day. This is comprehensive training developed by United Methodist ministers to turn their congregations into "saving stations" taking on the toughest problems of their communities.[46] On a rainy, dreary, cold Saturday morning I realized that 1 Corinthians 13 had little to do with the romantic love of our culture and everything to do with the kind of community selflessness these volunteers were gathering to train for. Paul's lines, which are usually heard with the overtone of romance, were actually written as a congregational ethic to guide their mission in a very tough seacoast town. Valentine's Day is the perfect day for training in community mobilization, antiviolence, substance abuse prevention, and health initiatives of all sorts. In fact, the more I think about it, Valentine's Day should be the national day of community mobilization to demonstrate the story of God's love as expressed through the sacrificial actions of people who believe in God.

Thanksgiving can be retold as a day of gratitude for the hospitality to immigrants as modeled by the Native Americans. This could be a day of special attention to show hospitality and justice to new immigrants and to others on the margins of our community.

In all of these attempts to turn the dominant story in a new direction, don't hide your light under a bushel (a nice story, by the way). Let the newspaper and other media know what you are doing. Use the occasion to extend a special invitation to appropriate people in the neighborhood or to relevant decisionmakers. For instance, give a special recognition plaque to the local welfare office for emulating the spirit of St. Valentine, to the state refugee coordinator on Thanksgiving, or to a local peace group on Mothers' Day.

Use the day to tell its story, to set a new context for old stories. But the day can also be a great day to demonstrate other strengths of the congregation: Valentine's Day is a good day for neighborhood visitation and accompaniment, Mother's Day for convening antiviolence colleagues. Preparing for the day can be an opportunity to connect people in the community interested in an issue by asking them to help you get the story right. Don't gather them to tell them something; rather, gather around an issue and provide them an opportunity to play a role in a new story of health, reformation, and renewal.

CHAPTER 6
STRENGTH TO
GIVE SANCTUARY

Oakhurst Baptist has been my church home for more than twenty years. I remember noticing that first Sunday morning, with the yellow light streaming into the wide open space of the sanctuary that there were too few people for comfort scattered among the pews. Both of my daughters were brought here within days of their birth, and they have learned almost everything they know about God from the people here. The building itself is sort of like a warehouse with awkwardly large windows. We were inordinately proud of the general dumpiness of the place, partly because it declared that we were not like those other congregations across town with their palatial recreation centers and shiny pulpits. And then last year I was asked to serve as co-chair of the fundraising committee to replace the part of the church building that had drifted from dumpy to dangerous. It was a shock to my self-image even to be asked to be on such a committee, and I quickly realized that I had no theology to go with a building committee. Because we always had the space and put almost no money into it, we did not have to think about how one of our strengths as a congregation is our physical space.

Safe Haven on a Dangerous Journey

It is modern to think of life as a journey and to seek a theology for the road. We like to think of ourselves as being on a journey and our congregation as fellow travelers. We tell about how God calls us to leave attachments that might hold us in place when we should be moving on. We like to hear about the God of the Damascus Road, who strikes down old beliefs and takes us on to new roads.

I don't know of a people more in love with the idea of going somewhere than the people of Oakhurst. We think it is almost always the right the thing to do—to go somewhere new, to lean across the next horizon, any horizon. We like that kind of a God and are happy to worship with those kind of people—the journeying kind. Given our vocabulary, you would expect us to buy a tent and camping gear instead of a building. Thus, it is a little strange to talk about our building as one of our strengths.

In reality, even while we talk about *going* places, we would not think a moment of *staying* anywhere else but this corner. When it gradually dawned on us that we had worn out the 1942 bricks and plumbing and kitchen equipment, we carefully calculated the cost of knocking our building this way and that to make room for new ramps so those of us now challenged by disabilities could fully participate and so all of us could be heated and cooled safely. That added up to a lot of money, so then we also calculated the cost of a new space—but still attached to this sanctuary, on the side, not the back. It never once occurred to us to go somewhere else.

Woody Allen says that 90 percent of success in life is showing up. That may be true for a congregation's role in community too. We are physically there. But where is "there"? There was a time when the answer was easy because the neighborhood and the congregation were comprised of nearly all the same people. Louis Miller, the pastor at the time our education building was completed, was famous for walking around the parish, tending his flock on foot. Today it would take a marathon runner—we're scattered across fifty miles of urban landscape. "There" is still a physical intersection where humans find each other, but often they have to drive or take the bus to do so.

As we thought about our physical space, we found ourselves think-ing about the inn in the story of the Good Samaritan. During Jesus' time an inn was much more than what we now think of as a hotel. It was a place where strangers could go for rest, but also for help and heal-ing and safety. There were no hospitals, so an inn often functioned like one, offering the amateur comfort that was the limit of medical assis-tance of the day. Jesus was born in the stable of an inn probably just like the one the Good Samaritan headed for when he tripped over the wounded traveler by the road.

We have always listened to the story with the ears of the Samaritan, thinking of ourselves helping people as we travel about on our busy adventures. But think about the inn and think about the innkeeper. For while many of us come and leave here on the way to somewhere else, a congregations' narrative is much more like that of an innkeeper and the sanctuary, an inn.

The history of Oakhurst is a repetitious tale of people coming to find a safe place on a dangerous, bruising journey. Prisoners and refugees, addicts and visionaries, seekers resting as their vision matures, elders still talking about hopes while their cohorts were sat-isfied with remembering. Some come here as a last place to serve, such as Ada Barker and the Pembertons, who came here in their elder years and stayed before dying. Others come as one of the first places to test their servant skills. Others simply grow faithfully old here, such as Patsy Peace, Rufus Hunnicutt, and a long stream of saints whose names gradually fade into the collective consciousness named Oakhurst.

From time to time we all are asked what we believe. Some of us with too much education or experience stumble at that question, quickly wandering off into conditional statements and complexity. But even those who are way too clever know the answer to the question, "Where can I come and see what you believe? Where can I see the intersection of faith and the physical stuff of human existence?" For years I have been able to say reflexively, "Come with me to this space on East Lake, to Oakhurst, and let me show you where people are fed, where ministries begin, where people invest their lives beyond the pull of mere self-interest." Amid the bricks and the stone and the wood, we remember what God and the believers before us have done here. Even when I have trouble articulating *what* I believe, it is easy to say *where* I believe. Look for yourself.

Where Spirituality Comes Alive

Only a small aspect of the congregation's capacity to give sanctuary is demonstrated in the big room that is usually called the "sanctuary," the worshiping space. The worship room is like the living room in one's home: It is where we display family memorabilia and welcome important friends. But, if you want to know what a family believes, you have to go down the hall and enter the kitchen, the bedrooms, the dining room, and the backyard.

The other part of the building is the real sanctuary, the safe and holy space where words turn toward deeds. When you move from words to deeds, you move from worship space to the working sanctuary, which is the library, the kitchen, the fellowship hall, the rooms for learning, convening, and singing. This is anything but abstraction—it is as tangible as plumbing. For words to become deeds, they need to find a place that is safe for sinners and seekers and servants, especially those who are wounded or unacceptable.

Ironically, for words to become deeds, they need a place for books and a place to safely talk about what is in the books—especially for those learning about God for the first time. They need a place for people to meet and plan.

These are all congregate experiences. Our working faith is not just an accumulation of individual thoughts; rather, it grows from a life that is more than any one or any several of us. We are not members of a congregation like we are members of other clubs or voluntary groups clustered around mere interests, such as tennis or gardening or politics. For while we do *choose* to be here, we are also *chosen* in a way that is quite unmodern, even tribal. Against the tide of individualism and private spirituality, God calls people together into a physical place, on a real corner amid sheetrock and lumber and plumbing. Beyond simplistic rationality, beyond consumer choosing, we sense that we are chosen to be here in a physical space, together as believers, follow-ers—a congregation.

From time to time the secular press discovers spirituality, and its members always seem surprised. Frequently they are fascinated by one of the by-products of spirituality, such as the documented link with individual health. *Time* magazine, for instance, described the scientific efforts to isolate the technologies of spirituality such as prayer and meditation and then run double-blind scientific tests to test the effica-cy of those practices. Not surprisingly, most of the tests show a positive relationship.[47] This is interesting but quite beside the point. If that was all there was to spirituality, we wouldn't need a building in which to gather, would we? We could just sit at home, pop in a spiritual video, and stimulate ourselves. Private, individualist spirituality is a lot like private, individualist sex—not very productive.

The lonely experience of spirituality is not all there is. Spirituality is nurtured and bears fruit in a congregation that can be found in a phys-ical space. It is exactly when I am weak, sick, in despair, and broken down that my faith is likely to be inadequate too. And what happens? In a congregation people pray for me, come to me, feed me, and send me cards to tell me they believe in my future, that they know God loves me even when I cannot believe it myself. And when I cannot find my way forward, or even find my way home again, the congregation—not my own little faith—holds me up and reminds me of who I am and who calls me by name. Even those of us who are currently doing OK want to be part of such a people, to be physically present where they gather, to raise children up in such a caring space.

Where Trust Grows and Shows

It may be obvious why a congregation needs physical space to exist. But how does the community beyond the congregation benefit from its sanctuary?

In his book *Trust*, Francis Fukuyama explores what determines which societies adapt most successfully to new technologies, new understanding, and new challenges of all kinds. He argues that the capacity to trust beyond the boundaries of blood family determines the capacity of a society to manage all the hard assets—the steel, asphalt, concrete, and cash. Economic performance depends on trusting social relationships. Any society that has to enforce compliance carries more overhead than one in which relationships voluntarily work together.[48] The hard part is that people only learn to trust by watching what takes shape in the open where they can touch it. Trust isn't shaped in the abstract, but in the tangible experience. In turn, it shapes the relationships that govern how people learn from one another and exchange money, food, and assistance. One critical place where these relationships come into focus is in the physical space of congregation, because this place claims to represent a dynamic that is more than raw financial power or physical force. It makes the strengths that community depends on visible; it represents them. Is it realistic to trust in anything other than money? Look at a congregation.

This is a severe question to ask in a time when those on the margins are despised, unpitied, and resented for their weakness, with mercy withheld self-righteously. It is even more important now that congregations offer tangible sanctuary against this tide of hardness, that our faith places reflect the God we have come to trust.

A community needs a space where that kind of loving God can be experienced both because the wounded need a place to rest and helping people need a place to serve. A congregation should look like a place where all can see for themselves that trust is justified. It should look like what it believes partly because humans tend to believe in what they see.

For instance, it is obvious from the sidewalk that sports are not Oakhurst's strong suit—we don't even have a basketball hoop in our parking lot. So with a few exceptions, we don't tend to attract athletes. If we built a gym and softball diamond, that might gradually change. Instead, we are a place that has attracted helping people, seekers, and lots of wounded people. We look like a place, even from the curb, for such folks, and so they find us.

The physical space also makes those strengths accessible and easy to find. Church buildings tend to stay put in a society where everything else moves around. Over time the places take on the qualities of the congregation and make them available to others. A meeting in the "faith place" sends a particular kind of welcome, even when the meeting is about something other than religion. A program or function, be it feeding or healing or teaching, takes on the space as its frame of reference. A congregational space is a very specific context in which to function. It is defined by the full life of the congregation, by its full presence in the life of the larger community. This isn't something that can be changed quickly by a new logo or communications effort. It depends on public relations, the relationships and connections with the public structures over time. A meeting about racial conflict held in a congregation that excluded African Americans for decades takes on the frame of hypocrisy or conflict. A meeting held in a bilingual congregation about changes in welfare law for immigrants takes on a frame of identification and compassion.

The building is often a tangible thing of value, a resource that can be shared for community good. Perhaps the neighborhood needs a clinic, a food pantry, a shelter, or a day-care center for children, elders, or those with HIV. It is unlikely that one congregation has all the people or funds necessary to staff such a program. Perhaps the building can be offered for use by other community organizations in collaboration. Often voluntary community change or social service organizations need office and meeting space that a congregation can make available. This is one way of redefining the space and in the process repositioning the congregation in the eyes of the community.

Sometimes the public health department looks at the underused rooms in a church building as potentially cheap space into which programs and services can be placed. The full value of the space is determined by what it represents in the community, which is determined not just by square footage, but by what has happened there over time. This requires more sophisticated vision than many bureaucrats may be used to. All space is not the same. Does it represent what you want it to represent? Is the lawn acres of chemicalized turf or is it a community garden? Is it worn and welcoming? Is it open and available to those who need it?

A congregation's building tends to slow down change like ballast slows a ship at sea. This can be bad if it restricts the flexibility of resources, such as when the debt on a building obligates future funds that may be needed for other missions. On the other hand, once the congregation is committed to a particular corner of the universe, it should be difficult to leave, to change one's mind. Because it is hard to move, a congregation may be willing to deal with the homeless, the poor, immigrants, elders, those living with HIV whose needs they might otherwise overlook.

The strengths of the congregation are not contained within its walls, but this is often the place where they are first accessible. The physical space of a congregation is a connecting point, not only to the resources of the congregation, but to all with which it is connected. The congregation functions a little like a permeable membrane around the resources and capacities of society for those who are on its outside or underside.

The trust that Fukuyama writes about is not intangible. It must exist in the world of touch and even taste. If you are hungry, even if you do not fully understand the food system, with its complexity of government, for-profit, and not-for-profit organizations, it is a good bet to head for a church or synagogue. Because over the years many other hungry people have gone to them and asked for food, about half of the congregations in America are prepared to feed you. They have bags of food on site to give away. They expect you to ask and are prepared to help. They likely know how the rest of the food system works too. This means they can frequently sort out what kind of other help you might be able to receive. If you are an immigrant, a church is a much safer place to sort through these questions than a school or other government agency that you suspect might feel constrained to turn you over to police or someone else unlikely to treat you as a human being.

The people in the synagogue are likely to know somebody at the food stamp office, the Women, Infant, and Children office, the Aid to Families with Dependent Children, or other social service agencies. They will certainly know people at the interfaith food bank. They are connected. And how do you know where to gain access to the web of connections? You head for the physical space that looks like a congregation, knock on the door, and hope for compassion. Maybe you are of the same faith; maybe not. The people in the building may be unknown except for the fact that they are found in a building dedicated to expressing the faith and have some accountability to that faith. That accountability is expressed in the most practical ways possible: making food available as Jesus would; being compassionate as any Rabbi should be; welcoming the poor and the prisoner as you expect a good Muslim to do.

When Oakhurst people decided to construct their building more than fifty years ago, the world was torn from Burma to Morocco by a war more violent and vast than anyone had ever imagined possible. More than a few of our own members died or returned wounded. Nobody knew the outcome or when it would end. However, the congregation trusted in the future even amid a global catastrophe and decided to build a space that would be safe for education and missions.

Any number of global catastrophes—global warming, extinction of species, hunger, human rights, and ethnic violence—beg us to veer toward despair and survival thinking. So, again, those of us at Oakhurst are going to build a new building for education and missions that will probably last into—not the twenty-first—but the twenty-second century. We cannot imagine that world. What cataclysms, amazement, knowledge? What fears and bloodshed, what heroes and saints? We can guess that there will be people on a journey then who will need a place to recover, to learn, to be nurtured. And we trust that there will be people to keep the inn who will need a place to serve. And we certainly trust that there will be a graceful God who will need a place to be found.

CHAPTER 7
STRENGTH TO BLESS

A HANDFUL OF WORSHIPERS GATHER down the road from the part of Winston-Salem, North Carolina, where Moravians have gathered for hundreds of years. On this Monday evening the kind of odd mixture that must surely delight God assembles—a few recovered and recovering addicts, a few recently released felons, a social activist pastor, and a scattering of members of one of sixty-five suburban congregations who sponsor Prodigals' Partners ministry, which offers rehabilitation support for men who live on site. The music is provided by a Mennonite rock violinist ."Blessed . . . ," they sing, "He's got you in the right place." The addicts, activists, and suburbanites relax in the blessing, receiving it as cool water for hearts burned by the hard changing times.

The service, which is led by the residents of the program, most of whom are chronic substance abusers, always opens with a time of gratitude in which every visitor is greeted by name with "We're glad you're here." The residents know that gratitude is the key to survival and that it is only kept alive by sharing it. The pastor, Jeff Coppage, explains, "The sponsoring groups always come to give, and they leave overwhelmed by what they receive. Here are guys with one foot in the grave, barely climbing out, expressing gratitude for making it another day. The rest of us have nearly lost touch because of our comfortable lives." Jeff learned as a missionary in Togo, West Africa, the blessing that comes from those who have suffered, from those who have lived their life of faith on the edge. The addicts face death on stark terms yet experience a spiritual vitality in their recovery that is just as vivid. Their response to this blessing, this hope, is gratitude, and they cannot but share it.

The residents stay in the program for fifteen months, although some leave as soon as they feel better, in a month or two. Jeff notes that everyone is impatient with how much time it takes to heal, to recover. It takes time for love to replace violence down deep, for gratitude to penetrate the shame.

Why Blessing?

This is how blessing comes to us if it comes at all: from one human to another in the name of all that lasts, in song, prayer, silence, word, touch, presence. We do not have the power to bless ourselves when we need it most, just on the edge of slipping, sliding away. The circularity of self-generated hope is too weak to stand against the serious doubts that wash over us, the crosscurrents that pull us this way and that. It is obvious that when we are isolated it is hard to say "no" to those things that may destroy us. The real problem is that in our time of weakness who can say "yes?" The power to bless exists between people when they gather at the intersection of human and holy. Only a community can say, "Bless you. Bless us. Yes. Yes."

Blessing is as hard to dissect as a breeze. Blessing is easier to see its absence, its opposite. It is not words, although they sometimes mark the way. It is not ceremony, although ceremony frequently makes blessing possible. It is not the space, although sometimes it is the portal.

The power to bless is not much help to those seeking to enlist congregations in their campaign to get people to do certain things. Those seeking the help of congregations for their own social programs don't want the power to bless; they want to borrow the power to persuade, simply substituting their own list of messages for those currently promoted by the preacher. One suspects that the recent interest in relating to religious structures on behalf of government and health institutions, such as hospitals, is a last gasp at trying to get people to comply. Health educators with instructions to communicate are frustrated that their brochures and public service announcements fail to change people's minds, much less their actions. "Maybe we can get the pastors to tell people what to do!" This has nothing to do with blessing and everything to do with manipulation. Actually, nobody in government, business, or faith groups has that kind of power anymore. Humans will not follow instructions. The power to bless rests on a more realistic foundation. Blessing sets people free, free to change, to untangle from their bondage. But blessing never prescribes, dictates, or manipulates.

Our fractured time is littered with relational debris from marriages and families. Many have grown calluses over their wounds, dampening their senses, guarding their hopes for wholeness. We are drowning in messages that promise blessing, but the blessing is attached to a product, an expensive experience, an addictive path, or some other manipulative allegiance. Many of the best paid people in business are dedicated to the task of turning our yearning for blessing into a consumer decision to buy whatever they happen to be selling, be it shoes, tires, cars, batteries, underwear, soda, or breast augmentation. And it is always pretty much the same blessing: youth, sex, wealth, options, power, energy—the future. "Buy this and you will turn back entropy, tame chaos, regain your lost choices."

The blessing we need cannot be sold or bought, only given through grace. This is why it can be found only in a community of sinners who have obviously needed grace themselves. It is hard to accept a blessing from people who are, on the surface at least, too pure to need one of their own. We need a place where the full complexity of our lives is welcome, forgiven, hoped for, included, blessed. It is a particular strength of congregations—some of them anyway—to do that.

Many congregations are not places of blessing. Ask the parents of a child with mental disabilities or any physical difference, and they will tell you of watching their child be blessed with words even as they are rejected by the actions of religious people. Talk to the homeless or jobless, the too old or odd, and they will tell you of congregations who pushed them down and away as if they feared the imperfect would pollute the fellowship. Words of blessing are experienced as damnation in such places and cast suspicion when the words are used elsewhere too.

If words are not the clue, how does one tell where to go to be blessed and not damned? I only know two clues. First, blessing pulls our attention to what is next; damning pulls us back toward what cannot be changed. Blessing evokes the life that seeks to break through, damning seeks to assign blame for brokenness.

The second clue is that blessing is honest. It includes the damage, loss, death, and brokenness and still says that at any point the turn toward hope is rewarded by the possibility of participation in, and alignment with, the flow of life that is God's grace. Damage is not undone or erased. But neither is it permitted to have the last word, to establish an unpayable debt, to remain final. In a way that remains partly a mystery, the power to bless incorporates all the damage and weaves it into a larger story of life, reclamation, *metanoia*—the reversal we could not purchase for ourselves.

This idea of blessing echoes with theological themes of justification and other issues that seem far removed from Monday morning. However, if you've ever awakened to a Monday morning alone, trapped in the debris of broken relationships and bad choices, you know there is nothing as desperately urgent as a way to begin again.

The power to bless is the power to move forward into an unknown future. Amid the violence and raw power of our systems, blessing seems as weak as a breeze, as shiftless as sand. What confounds the violent and the clever is their incapacity to do anything positive, creative, or new. The tools of media, violence, communication, and coordination are far beyond that which any of Machiavelli's princes could have dreamed. Yet none of these powers can dream of a new thing, compel creative sacrifice, or find the heart of meaning in the chaos.

Pseudo-Blessing

Those who seek to manipulate are not the only ones who misunderstand blessing. Many health and social service professionals know how others could improve their lives or at least prevent suffering by making better choices in line with better science. Over against hard data and good logic, blessing seems merely motivational. But data has no power to change behavior among people who have given up hope for themselves. Incremental changes in a meaningless life are hardly worth the trouble.

The power to bless is essential in times of great and fluid complexity. Mihaly Csikszentmihalyi sought to lay out a nontheological framework for a positive approach to life in his best-selling book, *Flow*. He discards the relevance of traditional religion, noting that "a vital new religion may one day arise again. In the meantime, those who seek consolation in existing churches often pay for their peace of mind with a tacit agreement to ignore a great deal of what is known about the way the world works."[49] His second book, *The Evolving Self*, sought to describe more carefully the path forward without dependence on outdated answers. Csikszentmihalyi wants the strengths of these congregations without what he regards as the quaint but delusional basis of their hope.

He hopes for the power of community that looks honestly into the ambiguity of the human situation and takes responsibility for engaging the challenges. He hopes for the emergence of wisdom that "deals not with the variable, superficial appearance of experience but tries to grasp the enduring universal truths that lie below it." He rejects the idea of God and of the religions that rest upon God, preferring "the comprehension of the underlying causes of reality, of the organic relationship between the various forces and processes in the universe, including the minds of men and women."[50]

In the end, Csikszentmihalyi's "fellowships of the future" look a great deal like graduate seminars, clearly lacking most of the powers a sustainable people of faith call on to engage a changing world. He knows that the "ideal social unit for accomplishing a task is a group small enough to allow intense face-to-face interaction, one in which members participate voluntarily, in which each person can contribute to a common goal by doing what he or she knows best." He regrets that "these days there aren't many opportunities to belong to such groups," because "the institutions in which we participate tend to be large, involuntary and anonymous."[51] Building around a faith in evolution and urging us to find meaning by helping to guide its unfolding direction, he knows that

> It is precisely because the unknowns are so great and dangerous that we require some manner of faith to choose our path and to give us courage. If we cannot believe that our existence is part of a meaningful, unfolding design, it will be difficult to maintain the resolve needed to make it come true. So even though faith in evolution does not require belief in a foreordained outcome, it does require trust in the unknown.[52]

Csikszentmihalyi is anything but hostile to the congregations that already exist by the thousands, doing exactly the hopeful, honest work of which he dreams. Indeed, he must know that the relatively barren concept of his "fellowships of the future" are unlikely to generate the courage, sacrifice, and resilience that it takes to seek the future. What he is missing is the capacity of a congregation to bless the complexity of life and in doing so renew our capacity to hope.

Clear Way for Hope

At the street level the power to bless is almost indistinguishable from the power to forgive. We are learning about this power, partly by sailing the deep waters of substance abuse and dangerous behaviors that now far outpace infectious diseases as the leading causes of death. Many have become tangled in the manipulative chemicals and techniques of our time. Many find themselves controlled by the very things they sought out to give them pleasure, energy, life. As long as we are isolated from something stronger, we are individually powerless amid these entanglements. Since a large part of the bondage is gradual self-loathing, we cannot generate the forgiveness to start over, even when we become free of the chemical bonds. Shame, fear, threats from outside ourselves only add to the loathing and bind us tighter. At some point we are saved only by a "yes" that is credible, authoritative, specific.

Artificial dependency is easy to see in individuals. It also dominates our social and political structures. Indeed, it may be even easier for addictive behavior to persist in communities because the power of the group to frame and interpret events and processes is hard for an individual to resist. A community can persist in oppression, denial, and blaming, shifting responsibility for decades. Communities can waste long-term assets on short-term pleasure, even resorting to self-destructive use of violence against its truth tellers. Consumption of goods—our "way of life"—can function for the community as addictive substances. In a short time the community, like any addict, is powerless before its dependency, repressing voices of shame and judgment. It needs a positive "yes" stronger than its bondage, an alternative that is as vivid as the self-destructive pattern that it knows leads to death.

It is debatable whether our current types of manipulation and bondage are more or less powerful than in earlier times. The media is more pervasive but government less capable; economic institutions more dominant but literacy far more widespread, with tools of communication and learning more readily available and poorly controlled. All tools of manipulation—from marketing to politics to intimidation—are self-limiting. The ceiling on their achievement is defined in advance by the limitation of the vision they seek to protect. An organization, be it a government or a corporation, cannot enforce compliance on phenomena it does not understand. What is very clear is that the most critical issues of the future depend not on compliance but on creativity; not on enforcing order but on saying "yes" to paths that are only just emerging.

The challenge is to nurture people of faith in the midst of these powerful, but not ultimately powerful, forces. All the manipulations and dependencies are only penultimate. They are supreme only in the absence of the ultimate, which only has the power to evoke hope, free us from lesser powers—in short, to bless.

The idea of a hopeful, loving universe floats in abstraction until we experience it as a blessing mediated in the community of other people.

Hope is the virtue, but the experience, the modality, is blessing, saying "yes" to what is and might be. Every positive action, sacrifice, and creative risk spring from this. The power to bless helps make it possible to move into the unknowable future, rather than settling back into the past. The crucial disciplines necessary to life in complexity are hope, expectancy, and anticipation. Deadly and painful mistakes are possible, even likely. Thus, a cheerful, self-generated enthusiasm will wilt before reality, maybe even before the first blows are felt.

A congregation dominated by fear and brittle externalities can hardly be a place of blessing and resiliency. The congregation's power to bless, like its power to frame and to convene, rests on the integrity of its life. It is basic Christian organizational theory: "How shall they know you? By the love among you."

Joe and Melanie Adair work with congregations in Atlanta neighborhoods deemed "at risk" on anyone's chart of problems. Yet these congregations are often the only viable, sustained social institutions alive in their neighborhoods. And they are struggling to live out a positive faith. The Adairs recognize that some kinds of religious faith evoke courage and creative power, while other styles of faith encourage the opposite. For decades experts in the psychology of religion have distinguished between intrinsic and extrinsic religion.[53] Intrinsic orientation uses faith as a guide to living and as the basis of meaning.

Intrinsic faith is open to mysticism but focuses on ethics in terms of love for neighbor, unselfishness, and on transcending one's own needs toward universal needs. Intrinsic faith is creative, open, and flexible, likely to be tolerant of different ideas. Not surprisingly, on a personal level, intrinsic faith is likely to mark people who recover more quickly from serious injuries or illness, and data suggest that they may live longer altogether.

Extrinsic faith is oriented toward rules and externalities, often selectively applied in response to threats that arise. Religion is valued because it seems useful to meet other needs. The faith is not experiential but tends to be reflected in the acceptance of social categories by sex, age, status, and external indicators. Not surprisingly, those people defined by extrinsic faith tend to fear death but, ironically, experience illness more frequently, and heal more slowly, especially from serious illnesses.

The Adairs know that congregations that promote a brittle faith oriented toward rigid categories are incapable of confronting the reality of their neighborhoods or even the complexity within their own membership. Such congregations want the power to prescribe answers, to lay out blueprints and rules, to still the chaos by enforcing a new order (actually, an old one). The answers do not take into account the complexity of human experience, the evolving menu of technical and social capacities. There is no way back into simplicity. A faith that holds out that promise fits a smaller and smaller fraction of lives.

The demand for compliance in advance of blessing pushes the likelihood of improved behavior even farther away. Anyone involved in substance abuse or its rehabilitation knows that the root of addiction lies in low self-esteem, the sense that one cannot qualify for blessing. Extrinsic faith, even when the rules are good, has no power to untangle complex brokenness, much less to move us with courage into a future that is unknowable and dangerous.

Implementing Blessing

The heart of congregations is their capacity to be fellowships of blessing, forgiveness, and encouragement. It is the power to evoke, not compel; to draw, not push. It is the only way forward, the only way to nurture the slender flame of hope and share it in the darkness. How does this happen? The implementation of blessing leads us quickly toward the accompanying strengths of prayer and persistence because it rests on faith, not on techniques. But a few things can be pointed out that are very specific to blessing in our confused time.

A Word of Love

First, although words are never enough, they are important. Many people have suffered indignity and worse with religious language ringing in their ears. Thus, many of our best words have become eroded or even reversed. But it is still important for people to hear, in the language of their mother tongue, that God created them in love and wants them to fulfill their created purpose. Say the words out loud.

Welcome and Include

Second, make sure the blessing pervades the congregation's public life. Be careful that the ceremonies and public occasions make use of all varieties of people present in the congregation. This makes it easy for people on the margins of the congregation to recognize that they are welcome and included. It also increases the probability that the ceremonies and words actually reflect the complexity of the lives of the members and those drawing near. Note important passages publicly that may otherwise be left in quiet. If a member who is a recovering alcoholic has stayed sober for three months, ask him if that can be offered up in thanks during the service. Likewise, announcing the finding of a job or an apartment or a foster home should be as natural as announcing a graduation. Gradually a congregation becomes a safe place where the real passages of our lives come into the open where the community can see them and bless them.

Walk with Hurting People

Third, go with people into their own complexity even if it carries them away for a time. The power of a congregation to accompany can lend special strength to blessing. If a broken or hurting person cannot summon the hope to come to the congregation, make sure that somebody from the congregation goes to him or her. People frequently leave the fellowship because they or "their type" have been rejected in some way. Others leave because their own weakness or pain does not resonate with others in the congregation, even though it may be shared widely. It is OK for people to leave, but it is not OK for them to drift away with the blessing of the congregation unsaid. A blessing never seeks to bind or control, and sometimes this must be tested by walking away. If people choose to walk away, send someone to walk a few steps down their path with them.

Expect Confusion

Fourth, expect confusion and complexity to grow within the congregation. The future breaks in full of disorder. If you become a place of blessing, you can expect those needing blessing to come. The problem is that you can't just welcome and bless the one or two types of social variance with which you are prepared to deal. An urban congregation functions amid population concentrations that make it likely that there is a quorum of every kind of person. You probably will see an ever-increasing diversity of people on the margins of acceptability, variously defined. Look at the narrative in Acts 2, and you will see congregations awash in social complexity that was thought by the proper society of the time to be downright odd, even subversive. On a practical basis, this can make organizing worship a challenge, managing the demands for pastoral counseling equally so. Organizing committees and program priorities also becomes a constant creative tension. You will deal, not with *issues* of homosexuality, race, disability, and ageism, but with *people* of different sexual experiences, families of different races, people with varied abilities, and people of all ages doing all sorts of things. Complexity will have faces.

Discern, Not Control

Fifth, the power to bless implies the power not to bless, which implies a judgment that precedes the yes or no. The fear of judgment is precisely the mark of extrinsic faith with all its pathologies. Blessing rests in the congregation, which brings its full complexity to the task of discernment and looks to the future in anticipation. This easily devolves into a means of control or defense and quickly becomes the power to diminish the confidence of others, especially the weak. We have all experienced control and indignity cloaked in religious vocabulary, sanctified by a congregation gathered around its fears, not its hopes.

Most formal tools of evaluation, such as those used within the health system, echo with this kind of power because they are used to force alignment with external standards. They assume (or are granted) a power rooted in penultimate authority, or less, maybe only money or privilege. They tend to count things and hold them against a simplistic standard of criteria that omits the complexity of human experience. The congregation's power to discern is less and more. It is less (and less feared) because it is unusual anymore for it to be involved directly in access to money or privilege. But it is much more when it brings into consideration a complex appreciation of what is actually going on, what is valuable, and what must be accounted for. A congregation's blessing will usually slow down, if not contradict, other more simplistic tools of evaluation.

In this sense, blessing can be conflictual, even confrontive, when it brings the reality of what is happening into view, out of silence. To bless actions and hopes can subvert more popular arrangements and challenge the existing powers. They may resist and fear, just like extrinsic religious organizations tend to fear and resist those oriented toward intrinsic faith. The power to bless, although as gentle as a breeze, threatens as it promises, and turns out to be the very rock on which hope finds its place to stand.

CHAPTER 8
STRENGTH TO PRAY

I N THE INTENSE LIGHT OF THE BROAD Inglewood streets the jewel-like sanctuary looks a little out of place. Everything within blocks is dusty beige, sunwashed, low-rent commercial or getting-by residential. Built in 1913 by Philip Hubert Frohman, who went on to design the National Cathedral in Washington, D.C., Holy Faith Episcopal Church for years anchored the wealthy white community in south Los Angeles. The neighborhoods, not so white these days, reflect a future without majorities, only minorities. Inside the congregation, Nigerians, Latinos, Anglos, and a handful of Asians gather to worship, sing, talk about health, and pray.

In times past there was a lot of money in the congregation. Now inside the Tudor manse everything is worn, hard-pressed to endure one more lap around a hectic schedule of committees and small groups. Before the worship service a dozen women—black, brown, yellow, white—and one Anglo male surround a nicked Formica table discussing health and prayer. Pamphlets on gun bans, walking, cooking, and blood screening are passed around. The energy is high because the after-church discussion groups on health issues have gone well in recent weeks. Twenty or thirty people—a significant percentage of the congregation—have stayed after service to join the meetings. And, with only a little bit of nervousness, the congregation has welcomed the health committee's idea of making healing prayer available during Communion. Plans are laid for the next Sunday's focus on prayer and healing, including several nurses sharing their experiences of how they have seen prayer incorporated in the hospital.

The sanctuary is slightly cool, light filtering through proper stained glass, settling gently on the stone and wood. The pews erupt with a cacophony of ethnic dress. The music, too, reflects intentional diversity that could clash, but instead blends Hispanic, African, and English flesh and breath into a formal liturgy. The kids think nothing of it, taking the remarkable blend as given. At the Communion rail, receiving the wafer in my palm and wine from the chalice, I glance from Ogo Mbelu's acolyte's robe to his Nikes, incongruous on the polished stone floor. Off to the side of the altar two women on the health committee pray a prayer of healing with one of the members, hand in hand.

Standing at the Intersection

Congregations pray. And the prayer makes and marks the difference between them and other voluntary forms of association.

How do congregations' strength to pray contribute to building healthy communities? Even though neighborhoods are different places because of the presence of praying organizations—congregations— prayer is not just a service provided to the community. It is the experienced intersection of the holy and human. But it is not only the experience, which cannot be turned on like electricity but must be sought; it is always something of a gift, a surprise, an act of grace. So prayer is also the human act of seeking out that intersection, whether at any given moment we experience anything or not.

In one sense, people can pray by themselves, alone, in whatever language and location they choose. God hears the prayer of any human who at any time or place forms a thought of hope or fear, pain or joy, and turns it toward the ultimate. God hears every prayer. Prayer is as personal as a fingerprint. And certainly, if one only knows prayer as a member of a prayer chorus, an observer of others' words and motions, prayer remains as a sunset to the colorblind. But at the very moment, in the circumstances in which we are most likely to want or need prayer, we are least capable of doing so by ourselves. When we barely believe at all, we seek out others, and hoping more than believing, pray.

Congregations do not leave prayer to whimsical chance. They gather people to pray and organize for the possibility of prayer. Informed by centuries of experience in every culture and situation, congregations systematically organize their space and time and actions so that there is the best possible chance of prayer happening.

Prayerful Humility Empowers

The intersection of God and human can never be exhaustively annotated in words. But because it usually happens when more than one person is present, words articulate the moment for fellow seekers.

I speak of prayer because that is the closest we come to God. But the activities at the intersection include not only those things we recognize as prayer, but also worship and any acknowledgment of God with us, the ultimate amid the temporary. The strength of the congregation includes a large menu of activities that include liturgy, song, poetry, and the intentional silence of a vigil. Sometimes, as during Holy Communion, music, movement, art and architecture, the glass, stone, wood, and fabric join the taste of the wafer and wine to draw us toward God and—can it be said?—draws God toward the moment.

Prayer is the reason congregations build sanctuaries and ministry centers and not just museums, performance studios, libraries, family life centers, and public meeting rooms. It is the difference, not just in function (they pray), but in why, how, and when they exist at all. We would all prefer to harvest the fruit of congregations without having to deal with the absurdities and mysteries that happen when humans try to talk to and about ultimate things. But prayer is what sets congregations apart. If they don't pray, they are something else, some other kind of voluntary association, but not a church, synagogue, temple, or mosque.

Prayer brings the full complexity of human experience into the space of God's full power and mystery. Despite thousands of years of experience, we are still learning new ways to pray and to pray together. For instance, until the last few years believers suffering with muscular dystrophy could not speak aloud, although they could pray and be present. But as I related earlier, two years ago Betty Thompson led us at Oakhurst in prayer for the first time using a speech augmentation device on the laptop computer bolted onto her wheelchair. Her modulated mechanical voice electrified the congregation and probably made the angels in heaven clap their hands in glee. Prayer circles and support groups operating on the Internet across boundaries of distance and time are also entirely new in the history of prayer.

The intersection of holy and human is also marked with questions. This has been a bloody and brutal century marked by the silence of the gas chambers, the firestorms of Dresden, the radioactive shadows of Hiroshima, and the deathly quiet of the Rwandan refugee camps. Prayer moves to the edge of that silence, distance, and emptiness and does not seek to cover it up with cheap words. Many who do not feel comfortable in a church stay away precisely because they respect the mystery and the words enough not to say them without meaning them. I have often felt resonant with a person outside the church who moved respectfully among the mystery, pain, and oddity of life. On the other hand, I am often estranged from those who share only the vocabulary of faith without any of the sense of complexity, humility, or awe. Prayer does not close off the questions; it turns them toward the ultimate. Prayer attends, waits, listens. And sometimes nothing obvious happens.

Inside a sanctuary people expect to find common meaning in the language that marks the turn toward God. But we live in an irreversibly pluralistic, multifaith and secular society. Even here silence, music, motion, and ceremony find common paths to point toward the holy. Communities that cannot pray in the same language find it possible— even urgent—to light candles and stand in silence holding hands at the sites of gun deaths of children.

Prayer does not turn mystery into clarity, into "unmystery." By definition, humans are overachieving but still highly limited creatures trying to sort out our place in a sweep of phenomena that our little words and concepts are unlikely to have fully grasped. There are always large companies of fools who use religious language and claim to have it all nailed down and sorted out, usually within a framework that turns out to be quite consistent with their financial security. The prophets regarded as wise across the centuries have always begun and ended with humility, and their prayers were humble.

I think of one Sunday morning when I got up early to walk the rocky path down into the Grand Canyon. I made it several miles down the trail and climbed up on a rock and listened to the nearly silent wind, which was moving gently through the morning just strongly enough to attract the attention of several hawks who were drifting in the wind about a hundred yards to the west and below. I tasted the dust on the wind thinking that it dated back to Creation, and that placed a different context on my forty-six-year-old aspirations and disappointments. I prayed with my eyes wide open, watching the vastness of time and process. But mostly I listened and thought that maybe I should spend more time watching and listening.

Congregations have the strength to prevent our understanding of complex social patterns from devolving into mechanical process or organizational technique. Today in Washington, D.C., twenty-something bureaucrats tinker with the fundamental linkages among citizens and the structures that bind us together. With confidence born of naïveté, they move the pieces around on spreadsheets, experimenting with millions of lives. In their schemes religious organizations are one of the pieces to be moved this way and that, with roles reassigned to fit what they regard as financial necessities (which, by the way, they seem to regard as less negotiable than any Marxist ever would). The strength of congregations, in their view, are mechanical ones related to their capacity to provide services, especially to people whom the rest of society is unwilling to pay for. The specifically religious activities are understood as the way the group is identified, sort of like a flag. Prayer is merely one of the techniques of persuasion that functions internally. Of course, religions have seen such social schemers come and go many times over the centuries. Congregations' true strength is rooted in the spiritual humility that prevents the humility of wisdom from devolving into clever cause-and-effect political rationalism. Congregations mark the confluence of human effort and more than human effort and warn us to beware of presumption. They are not a human mechanism designed to manipulate larger forces, but the opposite. Congregations are structures that help humans to come to the confluence with the holy and listen and respond appropriately with both mercy and justice. At that conference our eyes opened to the self-serving hypocrisy and injustice in ourselves and our world systems. We are made humble and alert in a way that opens the path forward.

Ironically, prayerful humility empowers in a way that political rationalism cannot. The pretense of human cleverness always collapses, brought low by any of the frailties that break our hearts and bodies easily. In contrast, a curious confidence grows when humility burns away the pretense so that we can align with deeper currents.

I think of Dr. George Ogle, a Methodist missionary to South Korea, who was thrown out of the country by the dictators. He dared to pray with the wives of union organizers who had been jailed as communists. Even worse, he prayed in public. The Korean secret service detained him and interrogated him for many sleepless hours, threatening violence even while they tried to undercut his theological ground by questioning his inappropriate arrogance. But George had never claimed that prayer made him clever. It did give him courage to open his eyes and heart and try to bring what he saw into the space before God. As a result, his disturbing prayers had aligned him with much deeper currents than the secret service even understood existed. Unable to break him, the Korean government threw Ogle and his family out of the country.

The Integrity of Prayer

It must be said that the most common abuse of prayer is perpetrated not by those outside the faith, but by those inside. Both dangerous and profound things happen when religious people turn toward the boundary with God without humility. The nonreligious world is appropriately appalled by some of our behavior—the inflated righteousness, the intellectual barrenness, the lack of respect for either human or divine. It is well-known that there are two reasons why people would not be in church: Either they have never been before or they have. Who can argue for the integrity of prayer after seeing a TV evangelist claim to have steered a hurricane with his broadcast beseeching? Or the spectacle of a multimillionaire athlete giving full credit to God for his victory (imagine God hearing the plea for help from the American stadium, dropping what he was doing in the Rwandan death camps). Even worse is the crass bleating of politicians trying to pull a veil of prayer over their pandering toward the rich and privileged. The list could go on to embarrassing length.

The shame, as well as strength, of faith communities has always been how they behave at the holy boundary and how they behaves toward others afterward. For much of this century leaders in various denominations have sought the way over the divisions between Christians, some preferring to sort out the theological issues, while others preferred to focus on common mission and ethics. In the summer of 1996 an ecumenical working group met in Johannesburg, South Africa, to bring the two streams of thinking together. They found themselves focusing on worship, prayer, and liturgy. "Liturgy, understood in this broad moral as well as devotional sense, is the principal dialogic encounter where God and human being meet: where the ecclesial body is knit together as a single cloth of narrative, teaching, repentance and forgiveness, confession and proclamation, prophecy and doxology." They continue, "It is indispensable to locate moral formation here at the heart of the church's expression of its intrinsic nature."[54] This is where faith is formed, not just expressed. Thus, all of the strengths of congregations are rooted here, made possible, and sustained.

The Johannesburg group confessed that liturgy,

> if not properly understood and acted out, can malform the church as readily as it can form it in faith. Liturgy and worship may well perpetuate or legitimate unjust arrangements both within and outside ecclesial boundaries.... Worship has sometimes been a rehearsal ground for violent expressions of nationalism against ethnic and religious minorities.[55]

Every murderous dictator seems to be able to find a religious leader willing to pray over the violence. "The possibility exists, as we have seen, that a given tradition of Christian formation becomes deformed or malformed by having internalized, given theological sanction to, and even worshiped local principalities and powers."[56]

Understandably, other institutions grow impatient with this unpredictable formation and malformation. They just want the congregations to spread a little bit of their religious ooze like an ointment onto the social pain, maybe give away a little free food and some medical services while the poor people are there. "Enough of mystery!" they say. "Let's strip away the mystical fluff and cut down to the well-defined process of group formation, meaning-making and social dynamics." Of course, you will no longer have a body that prays; you will no longer have a congregation or its strengths.

Part of the problem is that the issues that move us toward prayer are often late manifestations of very slow-moving phenomena. Prayers for environmental healing, dealing with patterns of global scale, are going to take some time! No less complex are prayers for the healing of relationships, tangled by years, maybe decades, or generations of malformation.

Prayer does not arrange circumstances to our preferences. Sometimes it does the opposite, undoing our comfortable arrangements and accommodations. It is not a way to align the universe with our needs or wishes. Rather, prayer opens us to alignment with patterns and flows that are larger. It is possible that that alignment will call into question the timid framework of our lives, enhancing the doubts, amplifying the tension, disturbing the lesser peace.

Manipulative prayer, like "applied science" seeks to control the power for one's own ends, good or bad. Deeper prayer, like research science, is willing to reject any preexisting assumptions or goals if they prove to be out of alignment with ultimate reality. Prayer and science are equally subversive to existing privileges and orthodoxies because they never honor the intermediary formulation as ultimate. Both assume that a greater reality lies beyond the current best articulation of truth. Prayer and science are both humble because they do not claim to shape reality; they conform to it.

This is disappointing to those who would like to enlist the power of congregations for their own ends. The government cannot simply enlist congregations into its schemes and "use" faith for its own ends. The congregations can't even manipulate faith for their own designs, much less rent them out to someone else. Indeed, those ends will always risk being subverted by faith, especially to the extent that it has been formed in the great prophetic traditions that emphasize just relationships as the most sure compass toward the holy.

Although those of us who live in faith groups have a lot to apologize for, the fact that the universe and the human relationship with it is mysterious is not one of them. People of faith do their best to describe what they collectively understand about phenomena that appear to stretch billions of years in all directions with a complexity and scale that make any attempt to articulate seem foolish. But we do attempt to find our place and behave respectfully, appropriately. For we sense that the ultimate spirit that moves is not anonymous, mechanical, or uncaring. So we respond, not just with awe or fear, but also with prayer.

Not Leaving Prayer to Chance

Congregations do not leave prayer to chance, although they approach it with humility. At its best, everything a congregation does and everything its members do inside and outside its walls reflect the awareness that the holy and human constantly intersect, whether we stop to pray out loud or not. Those people who maintain this sense of spirituality we call saints. Most of us come in and out of periods of sensitivity. It is useful for the less spiritually gifted of us to think of three aspects of how the strength of congregations to pray can be recognized for its implications for building health communities. Congregations attend to prayer at the personal, individual level; corporately; and also externally in the community.

Teaching Prayer

First, people expect congregations to be places where we learn to pray. We think of children learning to say grace, putting the palms of their hands together like little tents. And this is important. Children learn by watching, listening, absorbing as much of religious practice as they can understand. The most important modeling happens in the family, of course, but the congregation has a crucial secondary role to play and, in some cases, a primary one in families which, for one reason or another, do not help children to relate to God. Congregations do not teach prayer in the abstract. Rather, they seek out opportunities for children to participate in worship through song and prayer, experiencing themselves as part of a worshiping community in a universe that loves.

As we grow through life, we must constantly learn to pray in new ways, seeking depth to match the complexity of our experience. The passages and reverses of life literally force us to our knees and into silence. How does one pray when holding a newborn child, or when surprised by HIV, or when one's spouse leaves, or when one's child dies, or when one's factory closes, or when made incapable of speech by a stroke? My daughter, pushing the envelope of first grade development, and my mother, living in the frailty of old age, are both trying to learn how to pray.

A congregation teaches prayer by creating an open, honest space in which those further along the journey can serve as models and mentors for those of us tagging along behind. Sometimes experience makes some of us learn more quickly and deeply than others. I have not experienced the struggle of muscular dystrophy as has Betty Thompson. Predictably, her spirituality, refined and packed solid by years of frustration and difficulty, resonates with depth and strength that I have not acquired. When she prays, she teaches. A congregation finds ways for members to learn from each other, including opportunities to pray and to lend their experience of God in worship. The church takes us out of our daily lives through retreats, through experiences that help us mingle and learn from those of other traditions. It makes opportunities to learn from earlier saints and leaders by studying history and the great spiritual texts. Congregations do not leave learning to chance.

Healing Prayer

Second, congregations not only teach prayer, they actually pray for us and with us when we cannot do so adequately for ourselves. This is intimately linked to the strength to accompany, to be present. We travel for miles to be in worship in order that our small prayers might be amplified by the congregation. And when we cannot come, we hope the congregation will come to us and pray with us. When we are alone, in prison or trapped by age, we trust that others remember to pray. Even those who are estranged from membership expect believers and believing congregations to pray for them. And we do.

I do not want to lose the ambiguity and mystery of prayer by reducing it down to a mechanical activity that makes us feel better. But neither should we leave it hanging in the abstract. Congregations pray and are expected to do so even when they do not fully understand all of what is going on in that moment. Prayer does make a difference. Indeed, when objective researchers track health outcomes of many kinds and correlate them with religious practices including prayer and worship attendance, they find that it makes the same kind of statistical difference that socioeconomic status does on individual outcomes. The attempt to document the effect of prayer on individual health is at a primitive state because few scientific studies have even figured out what they are trying to describe, much less measure. But something happens. As they wait with curiosity for science to catch up, congregations pray with and for people.

As at Holy Faith Episcopal, a number of congregations directly link individual prayers with people to health concerns by offering the opportunity as part of regular services. It is important to make prayer as easy and natural to ask for as possible. This bridges the space between individual prayers and small groups that predictably share similar experiences and needs. Teachers and social service workers toil on the bleeding edge of social problems and tend to wear down. The Free Synagogue in Evanston, Illinois, holds a monthly prayer and healing service open to social service workers from their own membership and other congregations, Christian or Jewish. The small group gathers in song and silence and prayer in support of each other. Rabbi Knobel says the service is "for anybody who has a need for healing whether someone with an illness or someone who has some kind of spiritual pain." The service concentrates on silence and meditation. Light is an important element, and the service usually begins with the lighting of a candle and includes a short guided meditation on the theme of light.[57]

Group and Public Prayer

Congregations have a plethora of opportunities to lead people to the edge of the holy and help them learn to pray appropriately with people sharing their experiences. Traditional age-graded Sunday schools perform this purpose but only scratch the surface of ways to form meaningful small groups. Peace activists of all ages meet early on weekday mornings to pray together, for instance. Look for groups of people and offer to convene them for prayer regularly around common ground defined by work or concerns.

Small prayer groups can be important for deepening congregational life. They can also be an important opportunity to lend the unique competence of the congregation to the larger community. This draws on the strengths of the congregation to convene. It takes sensitivity, patience, and careful listening for congregational leaders to find a way to pray beyond their own space. The idea is to bring the intersection of human and holy as close as possible into the heart of people's real lives, opportunities, and fears. The simpler the format, the better. The key is creating a safe and respectful space, not filling it up with words that may or may not be meaningful. Paid clergy may not be the best persons to convene and lead the prayer groups. It is much better to train up a membership that is wise and sensitive enough to create these opportunities and allow people to recognize them as healthy.

Finally, it is crucial that congregations be present in the public spaces of society as they debate and negotiate how they live together. Religious groups may or may not be better informed on the data underlying the various debates. And we may or may not have uniquely relevant experience to bring to the discussion. We have to be who we are, communities that pray, that think that social relationships should be formed in light of ultimate things. Much of politics is about expediency and self-interest. Religious groups should bring a different quality of engagement that clearly reflects our grounding in humility, mercy, and justice.

CHAPTER 9
STRENGTH TO ENDURE

IT IS MODERN TO EXPECT RADICAL, RAPID CHANGE in almost everything that matters. But congregations move slowly, adapting at a different pace. That is the heart of the last gift congregations provide to their communities, the strength to endure. Nancy Ammerman thinks of congregations as living members of a community's social ecology—"living networks of meaning and activity, constructed by the individual and collective agents who inhabit and sustain them."[58] They adapt and change even as they breathe life into and depend on their neighborhoods. They accompany, convene, and connect. They story, bless, and give sanctuary. They pray. These strengths mingle and blend over time, uniquely reflecting the communities in which they are expressed. This flexible expression makes possible the final strength— to endure.

This different perspective on time is annoying, or at least confusing, to those who are not grounded in faith. The confusion stems from a different way of understanding time, brokenness, and endurance. Congregations generally see all three things in a way that strikes others as curious, a bit dim, certainly unmodern. Congregations are poorly designed to flow with every new current. Sometimes we are embarrassed about how slowly we move, how awkwardly we sing new songs.

But I think our different view of time is one of the great gifts to contribute to the community.

A Different Drummer

Like the other strengths, this is both less and more than what the community would like, because almost everyone else has a much shorter attention span, for example, election cycles, financial quarters, funding cycles of foundations, sports seasons, school years. We may be getting more stupid about time since so many things happen at a speed and distance that can hardly be imagined by a human. Congregations are built around a much slower cycle and recognize that the most important processes have not changed speeds appreciably. How long does it take to grow a human? About a generation, and, if anything, the maturation period is growing longer and longer as life becomes more complex, as it revolves more around continuous choice.

In California Native Americans built their economy on oak forests. Early white settlers took the trees for granted and did not understand the gentle and patient cultivation responsible for such a slow-growing process. Strong congregations cultivate their strengths over decades in order to build healthy communities. This different perception of time drives those operating on tighter cycles to distraction. Faith groups look lethargic or moribund, maybe even a little dense intellectually. That is how long it takes, even when it is regarded every week as the most important, urgent task at hand. It takes time to grow a human, a family, a congregation, a community. We can do all these quickly, of course, and we try to do so. Thus, we end up with childish adults who don't know who they are, with mutated families, with congregations exhibiting all the depth of a fast-food franchise, and with communities that abandon their inconvenient members without remorse. In their plodding way congregations stay on task and witness to a different cycle of healing.

Not that we don't dream impatiently. Think of how many hundreds of years we have heard:

The people walking in darkness
   have seen a great light;
on those living in the land of the shadow of death
   a light has dawned.
You have enlarged the nation
   and increased their joy;
they rejoice before you
   as people rejoice at the harvest,
as men rejoice
   when dividing the plunder.
For as in the day of Midian's defeat,
   you have shattered
the yoke that burdens them,
   the bar across their shoulders,
   the rod of their oppressor.
Every warrior's boot used in battle
   and every garment rolled in blood
will be destined for burning,
   will be fuel for the fire.
For to us a child is born,
   to us a son is given,
   and the government will be on his shoulders.
And he will be called
   Wonderful Counselor, Mighty God,
   Everlasting Father, Prince of Peace.
           —Isaiah 9:2-6 NIV

Those words were sung 2,600 years ago. How do you think Isaiah would feel if he were watching us in our modern gatherings: quiet, oddly clothed, sitting in rows on wooden benches two and a half millennia and an entire known world away from his familiar temple?

Nearly every generation since has been able to paint itself as "a people who walked in darkness." When these words were first spoken, Isaiah was concerned about Egypt and Assyria and his people caught in the treacherous darkness between them. We are no different. My little Oakhurst church sits a few blocks away from one of the poorest census tracts in Georgia. It is dark nearby. If you look back on the long trail of tears that stretches from Isaiah to our times, you have to admit that it is amazing that the hopeful Scriptures are read aloud at all. Surely Isaiah should be discretely put back in the box and left alone.

The theme of waiting and the frustrations thereof pervade Scripture and the history of the church. "Wait for me," God says. And almost with one voice throughout history faithful people say, "How long?"

Between Isaiah and us is the Gospel of John. It is not popular in academic circles to think well of John. After all, his sense of history is suspect and he is prone to mingle his words with those of Jesus like an opportunistic plagiarist. He uses allegory without precision. It is hard to tell what he believes and what he is arguing with. On the other hand, John at least knew that the messianic promise of Isaiah had not been fulfilled as the Jews, Christ's followers, or others had wished. By the time John wrote, Jerusalem was rubble and most Christian congregations were subjected to cycles of grim repression and were not good candidates for endurance.

John confronted the crisis of expectation by affirming that waiting is not all there is to faith. John understood what North Carolina Moravian congregations would later invent a love feast to proclaim and what congregations of different faiths all over the nation understand: "In him was life and the life was the light of [people]. The light shines in the darkness and the darkness has not overcome it" (John 1:4-5 RSV).

Some would say that John's theological affirmation lacks Isaiah's tough focus on governments and peace and wise policy. But he is also talking about verifiable fact and history. John looks at history and says that God has been here, is here, and will be here. Expectation is not all there is. There is more to come, but already we can say that we do not dwell in darkness anymore. The historic testimony of hundreds—indeed thousands—of years of those who have shared our faith is that the darkness has not put out the light. You can look it up. Better, just look around. There is no darkness in the world in which light does not shine and no darkness is capable of putting out the light. Any fool can look at history and see that it is so.

So There! Pass the Coffee

This confidence is not about passive expectation. We are waiting active-ly for God to consummate the creative task, and we are, frankly, unclear about how that will happen. In the meantime, we are still here hoping, feeding people, and trying to shape a human community to reflect God's hope for us. Thousands of years of despots and plagues and famines and wars and violence have not put out the light.

Moravian congregations laid claim to this humble, human-sized faith and made a festival out of it. Roughly 2,469 years after Isaiah, they built a rude little circle of logs in a pasture on the edge of a hostile wilderness that nobody had yet named North Carolina and had a feast that revolved around sweet coffee and a special kind of bread. Within walking distance of where Jeff Coppage's congregation of addicts now worships, the settlers held a party in the winter which everyone from the children to elders could enjoy and understand.

The Moravians were tough, practical people who knew about suffer-ing firsthand. They were a generation of darkness driven to extraordi-nary lengths to find a new place to wait for God. They read Isaiah and John, sang hymns, drank coffee, and ate bread to lift up the central fact of their lives: The light had come into the world, and no darkness the world had to throw at it was strong enough to put it out. "So there!" said the Moravians, "Pass the coffee."

I think Isaiah and John would like that. A lot. For that matter, so would Jesus and Mohammed, Buddha, and the Dalai Lama. I think we should too. I am an activist and drink my coffee on the run. However, there is time for the feeding, preaching, praying, listening, healing, and doing all we can to prevent suffering that mark God's community when it is waiting. But it is good that we should pause to remember that the light has come and no darkness has ever put it out.

Brokenness Makes for Endurance

The Bible is of mixed mind about breaking things, broken things, and the circumstances under which breaking happens. Brokenness draws

God's attention. Broken communities, bones, promises, families, hearts, nature systems, and cycles draw God's attention. We learn early in Sunday school through the gospel story of sin, cross, and resurrection that fixing brokenness is God's whole point. Eyes of faith recognize brokenness as the incompleteness that will be made whole one day. Thus, while brokenness litters our relationships and communities, the mark of failure is not the last word. For God is not finished and has not left us alone. Consequently, brokenness also marks the "not yet," the incomplete that God intends to complete, renew, redeem.

Another very annoying view of brokenness pervades not only the gospel but every religious body of thought. Brokenness is not just that which is to be fixed but also the very path toward wholeness. I wrote this chapter the week we broke ground for our new building at Oakhurst. I realized that "breaking ground" is not the name of the ceremony that launches a building, but the name of the place itself. This is where we come to break, to be broken open. Indeed, it is the reason we come, for through being broken we are made whole. Nothing new happens without breaking the old. This is the pervasive truth of eggs and omelets, wine and wineskins, seeds and gardens, birth and being born again, repentance and forgiveness.

I felt differently about this part of the gospel twenty years ago with no kids, no savings, and half an education. There was not so much to be broken. It was no big deal to pick up the pieces and rearrange them. I probably liked coming to worship better then, although I need it more now. I need to come to the breaking ground for God to have a chance at making me whole again. Maybe you know what I mean.

This brings us *back to* this brokenness that faith wants to make whole, but *away from* the false wholeness that faith wants to break open. We break ground even as we break bread so that we cannot possibly forget this truth that the world sees as paradox. It is no paradox, however, just basic straightforward gospel. We are made whole by God alone, for God so loved the world that he broke himself open so that we could be whole. All the rest is footnotes.

One Thing Endures

There is also a mixed message about endurance. Congregations are always intergenerational. They marry, bury, birth, and graduate in the same space month after month, year after year. The point is hard to miss: All of us will pass through the whole agenda and then hand our place on to somebody else. Whether it is my small church in Georgia or New Mount Calvary in South Los Angeles, we can think of the several thousand saints who have been in this space, most of whose names have long faded away. But they were here and in a way linger even now. I think of Carl Couch, a great saint who was already an old man when I first met him here. Few now know his name. When as a young member I prayed at his funeral, I felt like a young sapling must feel next to a great fallen oak. Of course, forest soil is made of such fallen oaks. Each of us should hope that one day when we fall, our lives will have been the kind that provide rich soil for those who spring up in those days we will not see. Again, there is no paradox here, just straight gospel. Strategies that rest on cleverness, violence, and power do not endure. The world is wired in such a way that endurance rests on humility and love. This is cold fact: Nothing that Carl Couch did for himself exists anymore, only what he did for others. Will it be any different for you or me? That is why we come to the congregation, the breaking ground: so that we can be broken open and participate in something that lasts, that truly matters, that endures.

As it is with members, so it is with congregations. As the social ecology changes, sometimes entire congregations fade and die away, no longer adapted or appropriate. Ammerman's research indicates that usually a new one more adapted to the new ecology rises in its place.[59] Sometimes the social skills, buildings, relational capital of the old congregation is recycled into new forms remaining part of the ecology. The form may change, even disappear entirely. Perhaps gifts of humility, love, sacrifice, service are never lost entirely. They build the soil in which community grows. They endure.

Congregations make enduring contributions to their communities because they are healing places, reconciling safe places of renewal and recovery. And they are places of learning, safe for asking questions and for discovery, and even for debate because, in humility, we know only in pieces and search for the rest. Humility and love endure.

Mihaly Csikszentmihalyi wrote about "fellowships of the future" with the courage and intelligence to engage the evolutionary chaos and build the future. That is what a congregation is. He comments that evolution does not rest on the transfer of material things from one generation to the next, but on the transfer and mutation of information. That's what DNA is, information about how to make a bear, a squid, or a human. Information that works well enough to get passed on endures.

This is a helpful way to think of congregations too. What congregational DNA will we pass on to these later witnesses that will endure? In faith groups, the DNA is embedded in the symbols, rituals, and habits of faith. These symbols and, indeed, most religious language, is more evocative, more thickly nuanced than any modern grammar. Many of the oldest symbols are shared from one faith to another—candles, water, baptism, silence, kneeling in prayer. This is the deep language that simpler, younger, less resilient organizations, such as governments or health departments find confusing. So be it. Members of faith groups in the twenty-third century will recognize the breaking of the bread and wine, that rich symbol thousands of years strong that is the heart of what we know is worth knowing.

Howard Clinebell calls for "reality based hope" capable of lending energy to heal communities and all that lives in them. These are not easy times, for as he points out, there is much to fear. "Reality-based hope is not the opposite or the absence of appropriate fear. It is hope that integrates the energy of this fear in a fresh synthesis that brings new strength to the person. Like tough love, this is tough hope. It is hope with muscles. It is hope grounded in a transcending spiritual reality that is its ultimate wellspring."[60]

There is a certain craziness at the heart of the universe that is captured in the symbols of reversal, the upside-down-ness of faith. All faith traditions look upon the urgent anxiety of our time with a slightly ironic smile knowing that all that counts is not counted in the modern calculus of probabilities. So we find time to accompany the lonely, to convene a meeting of neighbors, to connect someone in need with an organization that can help them. We expect God's work to go on, so we go on, too, patiently telling our stories as best we can and welcoming the hopeful and hurting into our safe space. We think we are witnessing the work of a loving God who has not given up, so we continue to offer up a touch, a word of blessing and hope. Because we are broken ourselves, we pray and sometimes seeing our faith, weak as it is, others find their way toward God, too. This all sounds so somber, dutiful, and full of heavy purpose. That is not at all what it feels like. It feels like life, surprising life.

I have heard it said more than once that you can tell if anything lively and new is happening in a research laboratory by the laughter. Humor and discovery are closely linked because both thrive on surprise. So does a living congregation. It turns out that God has hardwired a joke into the universe that you only get once you have been to the breaking ground and been flipped upside down. Like all humor, this cosmic joke rests on unexpected reversal, and it is a good one: Humility endures while pride dies in the dirt; sacrifice endures while acquisitiveness ends with death; knowledge remains incomplete while love fulfills and is never wasted. A laughing God nudges us in the ribs: "Do you get it?"

Congregations who get it accompany, convene, and connect. They give context and sanctuary. They bless and pray. They endure and build healthy communities that endure too.

APPENDIX

MOST OF THE EXAMPLES AND MODELS CITED HERE are drawn from projects or congregations that can be found through the Interfaith Health Program of the Carter Center. We work closely with grassroots activists, clergy, health professionals, and government partners with a primary mission of building the capacity for collaboration between people and organizations committed to improving community health. The program facilitates a national network of academic colleagues with expertise in various aspects of the intersection of faith and health.

The most current information is found on our Internet website, IHP-NET. At this writing the address is

http://www.ihpnet.org

and can also be found through the Carter Center homepage at

http://www.CARTER_CENTER@emory.edu

The website contains numerous models of promising practice for congregations and other organizations: training and course syllabi, speeches, and documents. We also maintain a lively discussion group online that anyone is welcome to join. Send an e-mail message to MAJORDOMO@synasoft.com with only this as the message

subscribe ihp-net <your e-mail address>

We welcome questions about implementing health activities.

Interfaith Health Program
The Carter Center
One Copenhill
Atlanta, Ga. 30307

Gary Gunderson
Gary R. Gunderson, Director of Operations
ggunder@emory.edu
The Carter Center/Interfaith Health Program
Voice: 404-614-3757
Fax: 404-420-5158

NOTES

1. Abraham Joshua Heschel, *Union Seminary Quarterly Review* 21, no. 2 (1966): 1.

2. Raymond R. Paloutzian and Lee A. Kirkpatrick, "The Scope of Religious Influences on Personal and Societal Well-Being," *Journal of Social Issues* 51, no. 2 (Summer 1995): 9.

3. Kenneth I. Maton and Elizabeth A. Wells, "Religion as a Community Resource for Well Being: Prevention, Healing and Empowerment Pathways," *Journal of Social Issues* 51, no. 2 (Summer 1995): 180.

4. Jim Wallis, *The Soul of Politics* (New York: Harcourt Brace and Company, 1995).

5. Loren B. Mead, *The Once and Future Church: Reinventing the Congregation for a New Mission Frontier* (Washington D.C.: Alban Institute, 1991), 27.

6. Martin Marty, "The Tradition of the Church in Health and Healing," *Church's Challenge in Health* (The Carter Center, Atlanta, Georgia, January 1989).

7. Walter Brueggemann, *Faithful Reading to Faithful Living* (Minneapolis: Fortress Press, 1991), 162.

8. Carol P. Tresolini, *Health Professions Education and Relationship Centered Care* (San Francisco: Fetzer Institute and the Pew Health Professions Commission, 1994), 37.

9. Alastair V Campbell, *Health as Liberation* (Cleveland, Ohio: The Pilgrim Press, 1995), 20.

10. Institute of Medicine Division of Health Promotion and Disease Prevention, *Improving Health in the Community* (Washington D.C.: National Academy Press, 1997), 41.

11. Ibid., 47

12. William Foege, "A Fair Start," *Faith and Health*, Fall 1995, 1.

13. B. G. Link and J. C. Phelan, "Understanding Sociodemographic Differences in

Health—The Role of Fundamental Social Causes," *American Journal of Public Health* 86, no. 4 (April 1996): 471–72.

14. Raynard S. Kingston and J. P. Smith, "Socioeconomic Status and Racial and Ethnic Differences in Functional Status Associated with Chronic Disease," *American Journal of Public Health* 87, no. 5 (May 1997): 805.

15. Bill Moyers, *Healing and The Mind* (New York: Doubleday, 1993); Daniel Goleman and Joel Gurin, editors, "Mind Body Medicine," in *Mind Body Medicine: How to Use Your Mind for Better Health* (New York: Consumer Reports Books, 1993).

16. Emily Martin, *Flexible Bodies* (Boston: Beacon Press, 1994).

17. William J. Strawbridge, Richard D. Cohen, and Sarah J. Shema, "Frequent Attendance at Religious Services and Mortality over 28 Years," *American Journal of Public Health* 87, no. 6 (June 1997): 957–61.

18. Council of Bishops of the United Methodist Church, "Children and Poverty: An Episcopal Initiative," Council of Bishops Meeting (Jekyll Island, Georgia, June 1996), 6.

19. Wallis, *The Soul of Politics*, xv.

20. Mead, *The Once and Future Church: Reinventing the Congregation for a New Mission Frontier*, 87.

21. Ibid., 5.

22. Mimi Kiser, *What if Every Congregation?* (Atlanta: The Carter Center, 1996).

23. Gary R. Gunderson, *Strong Partners: Realigning Religious Health Assets for Community Health* (Atlanta: The Carter Center, 1997).

24. Mead, *The Once and Future Church*, 7.

25. World Council of Churches Faith and Order Commission, "Costly Obedience: Toward an Ecumenical Communion of Moral Witnessing," Study Programme on Ecclesiology and Ethics: Third Consultation, Johannesburg, South Africa (Geneva: World Council of Churches, June 19–23 1996).

26. Margaret J. Wheatley, *Leadership and the New Science* (San Francisco: Berrett-Koehler Publishers, 1994), 151.

27. Wendy Lustbader, *Counting on Kindness* (New York: The Free Press, 1991), 180.

28. National Center for Health Statistics, *Health, United States, 1993* (Hyattsville, Md.: Public Health Service, 1994).

29. U.S. Bureau of the Census, *Historical Statistics of the United States, Colonial Times to 1970, Bicentennial Edition, Part 1* (Washington D.C.: U.S. Bureau of the Census, 1975).

30. Ken Dychtwalk, *Age Wave* (New York: Bantam Books, 1990), 38.

31. Catherine Hoffman and Dorothy P. Rice, Principle Investigators, "Chronic Care in America," in *Chronic Care in America: A 21st Century Challenge*, Prepared by The Institute for Health and Aging, University of California, San Francisco (Princeton N.J.: Robert Wood Johnson Foundation, 1996), 19.

32. Stephanie Coontz, *The Way We Never Were* (New York: Basic Books, 1992), 277.

33. Ibid., 253.

34. Ibid., 278.

35. Dychtwalk, *Age Wave*, 49.

36. Lustbader, *Counting on Kindness*, 179–80.

37. Gary Gunderson, William Foege, and Fred Smith, "Not Even One: A Report on the Crisis of Children and Firearms" (Atlanta: The Carter Center Interfaith Health Program, February 1994), 25.

38. Ibid.

39. Alan Geyer, "The Roots and Redemption of Violence," *Church and Society*, January 1995, 15.

40. Peter F. Drucker, *Post-Capitalist Society* (New York: HarperCollins Publishers, 1994), 210.

41. Granger E. Westberg, *The Parish Nurse* (Minneapolis: Augsburg, 1990).

42. John L. McKnight, "Redefining Community," *Kettering Review*, Summer 1996, 25.

43. Ibid., 27.

44. Ibid., 28.

45. Stephen L. Carter, *Integrity* (San Francisco: Basic Books, 1996), 7.

46. John R. Schol, *Communities of Shalom: Initial Consultation and Workshop* (New York: United Methodist Church General Board of Global Ministries, 1996).

47. Claudia Wallis, "Faith and Healing," *Time*, June 24, 1996, 58–64.

48. Francis Fukuyama, *Trust: The Social Virtues and the Creation of Prosperity* (New York: The Free Press, 1995).

49. Mihaly Csikszentmihalyi, *Flow* (Harper Perennial, 1990), 15.

50. Mihaly Csikszentmihalyi, *The Evolving Self* (San Francisco: HarperCollins Publishers, 1993), 242.

51. Ibid., 186.

52. Ibid., 191–92.

53. This has been written about extensively in academic circles. The following characteristics are drawn from Spika, Hood, and Gorsuch in *The Psychology of Religion*, 1985.

54. World Council of Churches Faith and Order Commission, "Costly Obedience: Toward an Ecumenical Communion of Moral Witnessing," paragraph 56.

55. Ibid., paragraph 57.

56. Ibid., paragraph 61.

57. Amy Greene, "The Spiritual Dimension," *Faith and Health* 1, no. 1 (Winter 1994): 6.

58. Nancy Tatom Ammerman, *Congregation and Community* (New Brunswick, N.J.: Rutgers University Press, 1997), 346.

59. Ibid., 347.

60. Howard Clinebell, *Ecotherapy* (Minneapolis: Fortress Press, 1996), 72.

INDEX